Civil Actions Again the Police

Supplement to Third Edition

AUSTRALIA
Law Book Co.
Sydney

CANADA and USA
Carswell
Toronto

HONG KONG
Sweet & Maxwell Asia

NEW ZEALAND
Brookers
Wellington

SINGAPORE and MALAYSIA
Sweet & Maxwell Asia
Singapore and Kuala Lumpur

Civil Actions Against the Police

Supplement to Third Edition

General Editors

Richard Clayton, QC, M.A. (Oxon), Visiting Fellow, Centre for
Public Law,
University of Cambridge
Barrister, of 39 Essex Street

and

Hugh Tomlinson, QC, B.A. (Oxon), M.A.(Sussex), Dip. Law (City)
Barrister, of Matrix Chambers

Contributing Editor

Mathew Purchase, B.A. (Oxon)
Barrister, of Matrix Chambers

THOMSON

TM

SWEET & MAXWELL

Published in 2005 by
Sweet & Maxwell Limited of 100 Avenue Road,
London, NW3 3PF
http://www.sweetandmaxwell.co.uk
Designed and typeset by J&L Composition, Filey, North Yorkshire
Printed in England by Athenaeum Press Ltd, Gateshead

No natural forests were destroyed to make this product;
only farmed timber was used and re-planted.

British Library Cataloguing in Publication Data

A CIP catalogue record for this book
is available from the British Library

ISBN 0-421-922-60-5

Preface

The Third Edition of *Civil Actions Against the Police* endeavoured to state the law as at September 1 2003. This Supplement covers developments over the two years since the Main Work was completed. This has been a period of continuing rapid change in the legal framework in which civil actions against the police are brought. There have been important changes to the statutory framework in which the police operate and a number of points have been clarified in the case law. The Independent Police Complaints Commission is now fully operational and new regulations and guidance have been produced. A number of specific points can be mentioned.

First, Pt 3 of the Serious Organised Crime and Police Act 2005 ("SOCPA") makes fundamental and controversial changes to police powers, making extensive amendments to both the Police and Criminal Evidence Act 1984 ("PACE") and the Police Reform Act 2002. The provisions enacted were foreshadowed by the comprehensive review of PACE in 2002, *Report of the Joint Home Office / Cabinet Office Review of PACE* (2002)[1] and the Home Office Consultation in 2004, *Policing: Modernising Police Powers to Meet Community Needs*.[2] Most importantly for the purposes of civil actions, ss.110 and 111 provide: new powers of arrest without warrant, which replace the powers previously contained in ss.24 and 25 of PACE. When these provisions come into force the distinction between "arrestable" and "non-arrestable offences"[3] will be abolished and there will be a general power of arrest for all offences, subject to a general test of "necessity".[4] Although the Government's professed aim was simplification[5] it seems likely that the "necessity" test will, in fact, make it more difficult to decide whether an arrest was lawful.[6] SOCPA makes a large number of other changes to PACE. Most of these are not yet in force. The Appendix to the Supplement contains a full copy of the relevant parts of the Act including all the amendments made by SOCPA.

Secondly, at the time when the Main Work was completed the new complaints system set up by the Police Reform Act 2002 was not yet in force. It became operational on April 1, 2004. There are new regulations relating to police complaints and discipline. The Police (Conduct) Regulations 2004 (SI

---

[1] Available at *www.homeoffice.gov.uk/docs/pacereview2002.pdf*.
[2] Available at *www.homeoffice.gov.uk/docs3/PolicingConsultation.pdf*.
[3] Itself a modernisation of the ancient common law distinction between "felonies" and "misdemeanours".
[4] See Supplement, para.5-049Bff, below.
[5] See *Policing: Modernising Police Powers to Meet Community Needs*, para.2.5.
[6] See Supplement, para.5-049D, below.

2004/645) revoke the previous regulations made under the Police Act 1996 and, together with the Police (Complaints and Misconduct) Regulations 2004 (SI 2004/643), set out the details of the new complaints system. The Independent Police Complaints Commission has issued Draft Statutory Guidance entitled *Making the new police complaints system work better.*[7] These developments are discussed in detail in Chapter 2 of the Supplement.

Third, the flow of new case law continues. We draw particular attention to a number of these cases. In *O'Brien v Chief Constable of South Wales*[8] the House of Lords upheld the decision of the Court of Appeal on the admissibility of similar fact evidence in police cases. The powers of the police in relation to breach of the peace have been considered in two cases. In *R (Laporte) v Chief Constable of Gloucestershire Constabulary*[9] held that it was lawful for the police to refuse to allow a coach party to travel to Fairford air base to protest against the war in Iraq when it was suspected some of that party intended to cause violence there. In the important first instance decision in *Austin v Commissioner of Police for the Metropolis*[10] Tugendhat J. held that the detention of a large group of people in Oxford Circus in London on May Day 2001 for several hours was lawful. This case contains extensive analysis of the relationship between the tort of false imprisonment and the right to liberty under Art.5 of the European Convention on Human Rights.

Police powers of arrest under PACE have been considered by the Court of Appeal on a number of occasions. In *Taylor v Chief Constable of Thames Valley Police*[11] the Court revisited the vexed question of the nature of the information which a police officer is obliged to give to a person on arrest under s.28(3). The case of *Cumming v Chief Constable of Northumbria Police*[12] deals with "reasonable grounds to suspect" and provides a further example of the low hurdle to be overcome by the police in establishing the lawfulness of an arrest. The nature of the "discretion" to make an arrest was considered in *Al-Fayed v Commissioner of Police for the Metropolis.*[13]

Actions against the police in negligence have been considered by both the Privy Council and the House of Lords. In *Attorney-General v Hartwell*[14] the Privy Council held that the police were liable for allowing an unstable probationary officer access to a gun with which he subsequently shot the claimant. There was no vicarious liability because the officer had abandoned his post and was on a vendetta of his own. This is one of the rare cases in which the police have been held liable in negligence for damage in fact caused by a third party. The Privy Council rejected the argument that public policy prevented the impo-

---

[7] *www.ipcc.gov.uk/stat_guidelines7_final.pdf*).
[8] [2005] 1 W.L.R. 1038; see Supplement, para.3-113, below.
[9] [2004] 2 All E.R. 874, see Supplement, para.4-089, below.
[10] [2005] EWHC QB 480, see Supplement, para.4-089B, below.
[11] [2004] 1 W.L.R. 3155, see Supplement, para.5-036, below.
[12] [2003] EWCA Civ 1844, see Supplement, para.5-071, below.
[13] [2004] EWCA Civ 1579, see Supplement, paras 5-049C and 5-086.
[14] [2004] 1 W.L.R. 1273, see Supplement, para.10-05 and 10-013.

sition of a duty of care.[15] In contrast, in *Brooks v Commissioner of Police for the Metropolis*[16] the House of Lords held that as a matter of public policy the police generally owed no duty of care to victims or witnesses in respect of their activities when investigating suspected crimes. It is noteworthy, however, that, several members of the House of Lords felt that "public policy arguments" should not prevent a proper analysis of the facts in less clear negligence claims against the police.

Important issues in police cases continue to be addressed in other jurisdictions. For example, there has been extensive analysis of the tort of malicious prosecution in the Canadian courts[17] in the Supreme Court of Canada has considered the elements of the tort of misfeasance in a public office.[18] We have tried to include the relevant recent case law from Canada, Australia, New Zealand and South Africa.

The law in the Supplement is stated as at August 1, 2005, but we have been able to add some later material. We would wish to express our particular thanks to Mathew Purchase of Matrix Chambers who was the Editor of this Supplement and whose energy and industry meant that it was ready for publication on schedule. Karon Monaghan again provided invaluable assistance in relation to Chapter 12. We would also like to thank the many friends and colleagues who have drawn our attention to cases and with whom we have discussed many of the points dealt with in this Supplement. The errors and omissions, of course, remain our responsibility.

Richard Clayton QC
39 Essex Street

Hugh Tomlinson QC
Matrix Chambers

September 1, 2005

---

[15] See Supplement, para.10-027A.
[16] [2005] 1 W.L.R. 1495, see Supplement, para.10-028.
[17] See Supplement, paras 8-026 and 8-066.
[18] *Estate of Odhavji v Woodhouse* [2003] SCC 69, see Supplement, para.11-020.

How To Use This Supplement

This is the First Supplement to the Third Edition of Civil Actions Against the Police, and has been compiled according to the structure of the main work.

At the beginning of each chapter of this Supplement, the mini table of contents from the main volume has been included. Where a heading in this table of contents has been marked with the symbol ■, this indicates that there is relevant information in the Supplement to which you should refer. Headings that have been introduced in this Supplement are indicated by the symbol □.

Within each chapter, updating information is referenced to the relevant paragraph in the main work. New paragraphs which have been introduced in this Supplement have been identified as, e.g. 2–022A. This enables references contained within these paragraphs to be identified in the tables included in this Supplement.

Short Contents

Table of Cases

Table of Statutes

Table of Statutory Instruments

Table of Civil Procedure Rules

Table of Council of Europe Materials

Table of Secondary Legislation of the European Communities

INTRODUCTION

Policing and the Citizen

LAW AND ORDER, TERRORISM AND POLICE POWERS

Policing methods

There were 142,795 "full-time equivalent police officers" in England and Wales   **I–010**
on March 31, 2005 and 223,426 full time equivalent staff in total. The increase
in the number of police officers from March 31, 2004 was 2,209 or 2 per cent.
This was the highest level ever recorded in England and Wales—for comparison, the 1995 figure was 127,222 "full time equivalent police officers": see *Police
Service Strength, England & Wales,* Home Office, March 31, 2005.

    There were actually fewer stops and searches in England and Wales in   **I–012**
2003–2004 than in 2002–2003: 738,016 in 2003–2004, compared with 869,164 in
2002–2003. The same proportion—13 per cent—led to arrest (see *Statistics on
Race and the Criminal Justice System 2004,* Home Office, 2004).

    The Home Office Review led to the passage of the Serious Organised Crime   **I–013**
and Police Act 2005 which extended police powers of arrest, entry and search,
and detention. These extensions of powers are considered in detail below (see,
in particular, paras 5–048 and 7–098). They have been the subject of criticism:
see, for example, the submissions to Parliament by Liberty (*Serious Organised
Crime and Police Bill: Liberty's briefing for the Second Reading in the House of
Commons,* December 2004), Justice (*Serious Organised Crime and Police Bill,*

Parts 1 and 2, Briefing for House of Lords Second Reading, March 2005) and
the Law Society (*Parliamentary Brief, Serious Organised Crime and Police Bill,
House of Commons Second Reading,* December 7, 2004) and the Parliamentary
Joint Committee on Human Rights (See *Scrutiny: First Progress Report,* 4th
Report of Session 2004–2005, HL Paper 26, HC 224 and *Scrutiny Fourth:
Progress Report,* 8th Report of Session 2004–2005, HL Paper 60, HC 388),
February 23, 2005), see also Prof. J.R. Spencer Q.C. "Extending the police state"
(2005) 155 N.L.J. 477.

Terrorism

I–014   These police powers have now been supplemented by the controversial
Prevention of Terrorism Act 2005, s.1 of which confers powers on the Secretary
of State to issue "control orders" against an individual if he has reasonable
grounds for suspecting that the individual is or has been involved in terrorism-
related activity and considers that it is necessary, for purposes connected with
protecting members of the public from a risk of terrorism, to make a control
order imposing obligations on that individual. If such an order would be incompatible with Art.5 of the European Convention on Human Rights, however, he
must apply to the court for it (prior to which a derogation from the Convention
would have to be made). In the event of such an application, a constable may
under s.5 of the Act arrest the individual concerned if he considers that the individual's arrest and detention is necessary to ensure that he is available to be
given notice of the order if it is made.

The Secretary of State has obligations under s.8 to consult with the chief
officer of a police force if the control order relates to a matter which is being or
would fall to be investigated by that police force. The chief officer must keep
any investigation under review for the duration of any control order imposed
upon the individual being investigated.

The latest figures provided by the Metropolitan Police in relation to civil
actions brought against them are:

Table 1: Civil actions against the Metropolitan Police, 2002–4

	2002–03	2003–04
Actions	146	124
Threatened actions	423	499

Table 2: Damages paid by the Metropolitan Police, 2002–4

	2002–03		2003–04	
	No of cases	Cost £k	No of cases	Cost £k
Before issue	85	419	98	800
Before trial	64	1107	65	1376
Court awards	9	828	3	65

CHAPTER 1

The Legal Status and Organisation of the Police

OFFICE, DUTIES AND POWERS OF THE CONSTABLE

The duties of the constable

n.38: The latest version of the Police Code of Conduct can be found in Sch.1 to the Police (Conduct) Regulations 2004 (SI 2004/645).   1–016

THE INSTITUTIONAL FRAMEWORK

The functions of the Secretary of State

When considering whether to exercise his power under s.42 of the Police Act 1996 to require a police authority to call for the chief constable to retire, the Secretary of State is required to have regard to the maintenance of the confidence of the public at large and not simply the public in the area of the force in question (see *R. (Secretary of State for the Home Department) v Humberside Police Force Authority and another* [2004] EWHC Admin 1642).   1–057

THE VICARIOUS RESPONSIBILITY OF CHIEF OFFICERS

Introduction

In *Coulter v Chief Constable of Dorset Police* [2005] 1 W.L.R. 130, the Court of Appeal held that it followed from the terms of s.88 of the Police Act 1996 that any costs recovered under a costs order made in the Chief Constable's favour were recovered for the benefit of the police authority.   1–066

Vicarious liability and special bodies of constables

In *Bernard v Attorney General of Jamaica* [2005] IRLR 398, the appellant had been shot in the head by an off duty police officer who was trying to push into a queue for a telephone. The shot was fired from the officer's service revolver. The appellant was subsequently arrested by the officer and handcuffed to his hospital bed. The Privy Council held that, applying *Lister v Hesley Hall*, the defendant was vicariously liable for the shooting. As in *Weir v Bettison* [2003] ICR 708, it was the purported assertion of police authority which led to the incident. The subsequent arrest was "retrospectant" evidence that suggested that the constable had purported to act as a policeman before the arrest. Finally,   1–073 the fact that the police authorities routinely permitted constables to take loaded service revolvers was a factor reinforcing the conclusion that there was vicarious liability.

A similar conclusion was reached in *Hutchinson v Commissioner of Police for the Metropolis* [2005] EWHC Q.B. 1660 in which Walker J. held that if the claimant had established that an off duty probationer constable had assaulted him after identifying herself as a police officer, the Commissioner would have been vicariously liable, she would have been "apparently acting as a constable, albeit one who was behaving badly" (at [154]).

The position may be different in cases where an off-duty constable does not put himself forward as a police officer or where an off-duty police officer *fails* to act. The Supreme Court of Queensland took the view in *Peat v Lin* [2004] QSC 219 that an off-duty constable who failed to act to prevent a breach of the peace was not thereby acting in the capacity of a constable so as to impose vicarious liability on the State.

See also *Mattis v Pollock (Trading as "Flamingos Nightclub")* [2004] 4 All E.R. 85, in which it was held that an employer was vicariously liable when a nightclub bouncer had stabbed a customer after having returned home to arm himself with a knife. The Court of Appeal said that the essential question was whether the assault was so closely connected with what the defendant had authorised or expected of the bouncer in the performance of his duties that the defendant should be held vicariously liable. The conduct of the bouncer was by no means unexpected because the defendant had encouraged him to perform his duties in an aggressive manner.

CHAPTER 2

Complaints Against the Police

THE CURRENT COMPLAINTS SYSTEM

Referrals to the Police Complaints Authority

2–012   The functions of the PCA were considered by the House of Lords in *R (Green) v Police Complaints Authority* [2004] 1 W.L.R. 725, in which it was claimed that that the disclosure of certain documents by the PCA was necessary for the proper discharge of its functions. Lord Rodger said that:

> "The Authority have not been given their functions to secure proper behaviour by police officers: that is the objective of good training, of force discipline, of codes of conduct and, ultimately, of the criminal law. Nor is it any part of the Authority's functions to see that wrongdoers are "brought to book" by being prosecuted. That is a matter for the independent prosecuting authorities. The aim of the Authority in carrying out their functions must be to satisfy the legitimate interests of both complainants and the wider public that the investigation of complaints against police officers, and any decisions on taking disciplinary proceedings should be, and should be seen to be, independent and thorough." (para.53).

Lord Carswell summarised the functions of the PCA as follows:

> "the *proper* discharge of the functions of the [PCA] involves fulfilling its objectives of maintaining and enhancing public confidence in the police and the proper administration of police services by endeavouring to ensure that the following ends are achieved: (a) police officers who behave in a way which falls below acceptable standards are not exempt from sanction but are duly subject to criminal and/or disciplinary proceedings; (b) members of the public, in particular, those who have a legitimate complaint against a police officer, can see that this is being done with a suitable degree of transparency and that there is no collusion in or tolerance of improper behaviour by officers; (c) the process is conducted in a manner which is fair both to complainants and to police offices" (para.78).

Post-investigation stage

2–020   A decision prior to the conclusion of an investigation can also be judicially reviewed in appropriate circumstances. In *R. (Wilkinson) v Police Complaints Authority and the Chief Constable of Merseyside Police* [2004] EWHC Admin 678, Gage J. held that the PCA had the power in certain circumstances to review and revoke a decision to dispense with the investigation of a complaint. The power to dispense with investigations was then contained in reg.3 of the Police

(Dispensation From Requirement to Investigate Complaints) Regulations 1985 (SI 1985/672); it is now to be found in reg.3 of the Police (Complaints and Misconduct) Regulations 2004.

THE INDEPENDENT POLICE COMPLAINTS COMMISSION

Functions and powers

Section 10 of the Police Reform Act 2002 ("PRA") sets out the functions of the new Independent Police Complaints Commission, which replaced the PCA on March 31, 2004. These are explored in the Draft Guidance prepared by the IPCC (*Making the new police complaints system work better*) at pp.7 and 8: see *www.ipcc.gov.uk/stat_guidelines7_final.pdf*. While the IPCC has a more active role to play in investigating complaints than the PCA did, its general functions are similar to those of the PCA.   2–021

The Police (Conduct) Regulations 2004 (SI 2004/645) revoke the previous regulations made under the Police Act 1996 and, together with the Police (Complaints and Misconduct) Regulations 2004 (SI 2004/643), set out the details of the new complaints system. Both sets of regulations came into force on April 1, 2004. Any complaint made on or after that date is dealt with under the new system, unless it relates to conduct of a special constable which occurred or commenced before April 1, 2004, in which case the old regulations continue to apply: see the Police (Conduct) Regulations 2004, reg.2. The old regulations continue to apply to any complaint received *before* April 1, 2004.   2–022

The IPCC has power under s.22 of the PRA to issue Guidance which must be taken into account by every person exercising or performing the powers and duties to which the guidance relates and to whom the guidance has been issued. At the time of writing the IPCC had reached the stage of issuing Draft Statutory Guidance entitled *Making the new police complaints system work better*, (*www.ipcc.gov.uk/stat_guidelines7_final.pdf*). This does not yet have the status of Guidance issued under s.22, but is a useful guide to the kind of approach likely to be taken by the IPCC.   2–022A

Disclosure

The duty to keep the complainant and other interested parties informed applies not just to the IPCC when it is conducting or managing an investigation, but also to an appropriate authority conducting investigations on its own behalf or under the supervision of the IPCC: see PRA, ss.20(2) and 21(7).   2–023

2–023A   The Police (Complaints and Misconduct) Regulations 2004 contain further provisions on the duty to keep the claimant informed. Regulation 11 stipulates the manner in which the duties to provide information are to be performed. The IPCC or the appropriate authority must inform the complainant or the interested party of the progress of the investigation promptly and, it would seem, should update him every four weeks (reg.11(2)(a) and 11(3)(a) are not entirely clear, but this is the view of the IPCC in its Draft Guidance at p.23.) The complainant or interested party must be informed of any provisional findings as frequently as the IPCC or appropriate authority deems appropriate in order for the complainant to be kept properly informed. Upon completion of the investigation, the complainant is entitled to be notified of the dates on which the final report is likely to be submitted and on which notification under paras 23(9) or 24(7) of Sch.3 to the PRA is likely to be given. He may also request—or be invited to attend—a meeting with the IPCC or appropriate authority at this stage. The IPCC or the appropriate authority must also notify the complainant or interested person of the outcome of any misconduct hearing conducted as a result of the investigation.

2–023B   Any notification should be given in writing, with two exceptions (see regs 11(8) and 27(1)): first, information given in a meeting may—of course—be given orally, but should be followed by a written record; second, if the IPCC or investigating authority considers that the investigation has made minimal or no progress since the last notification, a new notification need not be in writing. The Draft Guidance suggests that there is a further exception: notifications need not be given in writing if the complainant agrees to another method (p.23). However, while such an agreement may well undermine any challenge to a failure to give a notification in writing, this approach does not appear to be permitted by the Police (Complaints and Misconduct) Regulations 2004.

2–023C   The time limits in the Police (Complaints and Misconduct) Regulations 2004 are binding unless exceptional circumstances prevent them being complied with (reg.27(2)).

2–023D   Regulation 12 provides that the general duty to keep the complainant informed does not apply where, in the opinion of the IPCC or the appropriate authority, the non-disclosure of information is necessary:

- for the purpose of preventing premature or inappropriate disclosure of information relevant to actual or prospective criminal proceedings,

- in the interests of national security,

- for the prevention or detection of crime or the apprehension or prosecution of offenders,

- on proportionality grounds, or

- in the public interest.

Such non-disclosure is only "necessary" if the IPCC or the appropriate authority is satisfied that there is a real risk that disclosure would have a significant adverse effect on the ground relied on.

The new duty to keep the complainant informed in effect reverses the previous position under s.80 of the Police Act 1996: previously, information was *not* to be disclosed unless one of the exceptions under s.80 applied. This was the basis of the decision of the House of Lords in R. *(Green) v Police Complaints Authority* [2004] 1 W.L.R. 725, which upheld the decision of the Court of Appeal on somewhat narrower grounds. Lord Rodger held that the disclosure of witness statements and experts' reports was not necessary for the proper discharge of the functions of the PCA and therefore did not fall within one of the exceptions in s.80. 2–026

Now, however, information *must be* provided unless one of the exceptions under reg.12 of the Police (Complaints and Misconduct) Regulations 2004 applies. This is an important change of emphasis, but the extent of its impact remains to be seen. It seems unlikely that it would have made a difference to the outcome on the facts of the *Green* case, since the material requested by the claimant related to actual or possible criminal proceedings, which is an exception to disclosure listed in reg.12(1)(a). In fact, since the House of Lords in *Green* considered that a person conducting an investigation of a complaint against a police officer "will generally be conducting a criminal investigation" and that the disclosure of material relating to it would be inappropriate (paras 56 and 80), it seems likely that reg.12(1)(a) will often be relied on to prevent detailed disclosure in some complaints. 2–026B

The Draft Guidance does not discuss the disclosure of any particular documents other than the investigation report. It suggests (p.24) that the disclosure of the report is the best way of providing details to the complainant of the findings of the investigation report and any action to be taken (which must be done, either in writing or at a meeting, see paras 23(9) and 24(7) of Sch.3 to the PRA and reg.11(5) and (8) of the Police (Complaints and Misconduct) Regulations 2004). It thus seems likely that it will be disclosed in many cases. However, disclosure of the report is, like all disclosure, subject to reg.12 of the Police (Complaints and Misconduct) Regulations 2004. The Draft Guidance states (p.26) that "generally an investigation report will not be disclosed in advance of a decision to prosecute", unless there is no real prospect of a criminal prosecution or in exceptional circumstances where "there is no real prospect of . . . difficulties arising". When a criminal prosecution is unlikely or concluded but disciplinary proceedings are pending, then the Draft Guidance recommends "a risk assessment in individual cases". 2–026C

Certain documents have to be disclosed under the Police (Complaints and Misconduct) Regulations 2004: a copy of the complaint, for example, must be provided by virtue of reg.14 to both the complainant and the person complained against. However, it seems likely that the approach to disclosure of other documents will be similar to the proposed approach of the IPCC to disclosure of the report. 2–026D

Outline of the system

2–029   The Draft Guidance states that complaints may be made *via* approved Complaints Access Points, non-police organisations with experience of the complaints system, or any third party, provided the complainant give written permission.

2–032   Complaints which the police must refer to the IPCC are now set out in para.4 of Sch.3 to the PRA and reg.2 of the Police (Complaints and Misconduct) Regulations 2004. They are:

- conduct resulting in death or serious injury,

- a serious assault (as defined in guidance issued by the IPCC),

- a serious sexual offence (as defined in guidance issued by the IPCC),

- serious corruption (as defined in guidance issued by the IPCC),

- a criminal offence or behaviour which is liable to lead to a disciplinary sanction and was aggravated by discriminatory behaviour on grounds of race, sex, religion or other status identified in guidance issued by the IPCC,

- a serious arrestable offence within the meaning of s.116 of PACE,

- other complaints arising from incidents in which one of the above is also alleged.

2–032A   It should be noted that, from a date to be appointed by the Secretary of State, s.116 of PACE will no longer have effect: see para.43(12) of Sch.7 to and s.178 of the Serious Organised Crime and Police Act 2005. It is not clear what changes will be made to reg.2 of the Police (Complaints and Misconduct) Regulations 2004 to accommodate this.

          The police must also refer these matters to the IPCC if there is no complaint but the matter is brought to their attention in another way: see the PRA, para.13 and the Police (Complaints and Misconduct) Regulations 2004, reg.5.

MAKING AN ALLEGATION OF MISCONDUCT

Complaints

2–044   The procedure for appeals against an appropriate authority's refusal to record a complaint is set out in reg.8 of the Police (Complaints and Misconduct) Regulations 2004. The complainant must appeal in writing within 28 days of notification of the refusal, setting out:

- details of the complaint,

- the date on which the complaint was made,

- the name of the police force or police authority which gave notification of the failure,

- the grounds for the appeal, and

- the date on which the complainant was notified of the determination or of the failure to record the complaint.

The IPCC must determine the outcome of the appeal as soon as practicable.

Conduct matters

The conduct matters which must be recorded are: 2–050

- a serious assault, as defined in the Guidance,

- a serious sexual offence, as defined in the Guidance,

- serious corruption, as defined in the Guidance,

- a criminal offence or behaviour which is liable to lead to a disciplinary sanction and which in either case was aggravated by discriminatory behaviour on the grounds of a person's race, sex, religion, or other status identified by the Guidance,

- a serious arrestable offence within the meaning of s.116 of PACE,

- other conduct alleged to have taken place in the same incident in which one of the above is also alleged,

- conduct resulting in death or serious injury,

- conduct which has adversely affected a member of the public,

- conduct whose gravity or other exceptional circumstances make it appropriate to record the matter.

See the PRA, Sch.3, para.11 and the Police (Complaints and Misconduct) Regulations 2004, reg.5(1). (Note that, from a date to be appointed by the Secretary of State, s.116 of PACE will no longer have effect: see para.43(12) of Sch.7 to and s.178 of the Serious Organised Crime and Police Act 2005. It is not clear what changes will be made to reg.5 of the Police (Complaints and Misconduct) Regulations 2004 to accommodate this.)

The conduct matters which must be referred to the IPCC are the same as   2–052
those listed in Supplement, para.2–032, above.

Complaints against senior officers

2–054   The Police (Conduct) (Senior Officers) Regulations 1999 no longer apply, subject to the transitional provisions outlined in para.2–005 above. Senior officers are now subject to the same regulations as other officers. However, there remain some differences in the way they are treated. For example, a sanction may be imposed on a senior officer without a hearing if he accepts that his conduct did not meet the appropriate standard: Police (Conduct) Regulations 2004, reg.13. It appears that, in such a case, no reference to the matter would be made on the officer's personal record: see reg.11(7). If a hearing does take place, the senior officer's costs will be met from the police fund under reg.39; there is no equivalent provision in relation to junior officers.

Referrals to the IPCC

2–055   For the matters which must be referred to the IPCC, see Supplement, para.2–032.
2–056   Examples in the Draft Guidance of cases where the IPCC would expect voluntary referral include:

- "near misses", where death or serious injury nearly occurred,

- discharge of firearms or Tasers,

- allegations of domestic violence.

(Draft Guidance, p.28). The Draft Guidance also includes serious arrestable offences and discrimination in the list, but these would be mandatory referrals even if no complaint was made (see reg.5 of the Police (Complaints and Misconduct) Regulations 2004).
2–063   Regulation 6 of the Police (Complaints and Misconduct) Regulations 2004 sets out the conditions on which the IPCC can impose requirements on the conduct of investigations supervised by it. It may impose any reasonable requirements as appear to it to be necessary, but (i) the permission of the Director of Public Prosecutions is required before the IPCC may impose any requirement relating to the obtaining or preservation of evidence of a criminal offence in an investigation where the possibility of criminal proceedings arises, and (ii) the IPCC must consult with and have regard to representations made by a chief officer before imposing a requirement relating to the resources to be made available by the chief officer for the purposes of an investigation:
2–064   The Draft Guidance notes at p.28 that, at the time of consultation, the only matters which the IPCC had reserved to itself were those arising from counter-terrorism operations.
2–065   The IPCC may discontinue an investigation into a complaint:

- in which the complainant refuses to co-operate to the extent that the IPCC considers that it is not reasonably practicable to proceed with the investigation,

- which the complainant has agreed may be subjected to local resolution,

- which the IPCC considers is vexatious, oppressive or otherwise an abuse of the procedures for dealing with complaints or conduct matters,

- which is repetitious (that is, substantially the same as a previous complaint or conduct matter which was appropriately dealt with, raising no fresh allegations or fresh evidence),

- which the IPCC otherwise considers is such as to make it not reasonably practicable to proceed with the investigation.

See the Police (Complains and Misconduct) regulations 2004, regs 3(3) and 7.

COMPLAINTS PROCEDURE

Local resolution

The Police (Complaints) (Informal Resolution) Regulations 1985 remain in force but have no role to play under the new complaints scheme. Regulation 4 of the Police (Complaints and Misconduct) Regulations 2004 provides that the procedures available for local resolution are any procedures which are approved by the IPCC, subject to certain minimum requirements, which include the following: 2–070

- the person appointed to deal with the matter shall as soon as practicable give the complainant and the person complained against the opportunity to comment on the complaint,

- a record shall be made of the outcome of the procedure, and

- the record shall be sent to the person complained against and, if the complainant applies for a copy within three months of the date of the local resolution of the complaint, to him.

The IPCC appears to be disinclined to provide much greater direction than this. It has issued a document entitled *Operational Advice Notes to Police Forces: Local Resolution of Complaints* (which can be found at (*www.ipcc.gov.uk/local_resolution1702.pdf*). It sets out the general principles the IPCC expects to see followed—such as coherence and consistency, respect for people, and efficiency—but provides little guidance as to the precise mechanisms to be followed. The Draft Guidance also gives little assistance as to 2–070A particular procedures to be followed and seems content to leave the details to individual police forces. At p.19 it states:

"Local Resolution is an umbrella process that can be used for discussing issues, providing information, apologising or sometimes for bringing the complainant and the person they have complained about to talk the matter through."

It suggests a timescale of 28 days, although recognises that police forces may need longer than this to resolve complex cases or to satisfy particular complainants. The Draft Guidance strongly encourages the use of local resolution:

"Most people who make complaints about the police have them settled locally by the force, for example by the station inspector or civilian staff manager or at Basic Command Unit (BCU) level.
    The IPCC believes that even more complaints can be dealt with at this level—Local Resolution is usually the most appropriate and proportionate response." (p.18)

2–070B   The Draft Guidance notes that "successful use of Local Resolution depends on a complainant's informed consent"; this is true not only as a matter of practice, of course, but also as a matter of law: see the PRA, Sch.3, para.6(2)(a). Complainants would be well advised to ensure before giving their consent to the use of local resolution (which cannot be withdrawn once given (PRA, Sch.3, para.6(7)) that they are provided by the police force in question with a procedure to be followed with which they are happy (and ideally one which has been approved by the IPCC). Complainants can only appeal against a local resolution's failure to comply with procedural requirements (PRA, Sch.3, para.9(2)); as discussed above, there are few "procedural requirements" set out in the legislation or the Guidance and it accordingly seems likely that the police force's own proposed procedure will be of particular importance here. The IPCC has indicated that in dealing with appeals, it will consider the type and level of information given to the complainant, whether the complainant's consent was informed, what other options were realistically available and whether the process explained at the outset was actually carried out: see the Draft Guidance, p.20.

Investigation of complaints

2–077   The Police (Conduct) Regulations 2004 make further provisions for the investigation of complaints. If the complaint does not involve a senior officer (a chief constable, a deputy chief constable or an assistant chief constable or, in London, any officer above the rank of commander: reg.3) the following procedure applies.

Where the complaint is being investigated by the appropriate authority on its own behalf, the chief officer may appoint an officer of at least the rank of chief inspector, at least one rank above the officer complained against, and in the same force as the officer complained against, to supervise the investigation: reg.7. The supervising officer may in turn appoint an investigating officer who is: (a) of at least the rank of sergeant (unless the officer complained against is a superintendent or chief superintendent, in which case the investigating officer must be of a least the rank of commander or assistant chief constable), (b) of at least the same rank as the officer complained against, and (c) a member of the same police force as the officer complained against (unless a chief officer of another force agrees to provide an investigating officer): reg.8. The supervising officer need not appoint an investigating officer until he is satisfied that there is something which properly requires an investigation (see *R. (Ashton) v Chief Constable of West Yorkshire* [2005] EWHC Admin 975 at [20]). Neither the supervising nor the investigating officer should be an interested party.

Where the officer is a senior officer, the following procedure applies, again under reg.8. The appropriate authority has to refer the matter to an investigating officer unless it decides no proceedings need be taken. The investigating officer is appointed by the appropriate authority and must be of at least the same rank as the officer complained of unless the officer complained against is the Commissioner or Deputy Commissioner of Police of the Metropolis, in which case he is appointed by the Secretary of State and need not be a police officer at all. In either case, the investigating officer may not be the chief officer concerned, a member of the same force as the officer complained of (or, if he is a member of the Metropolitan Police, from the same division), or an interested party.   2–077A

Regulation 8(3) which states that reg.8(1) and (2) do not apply where any of paras 16–19 of Sch.3 to the PRA apply, if read literally, would mean that an investigating officer would never be appointed, because paras 16–19 detail the only four investigative options available: see regs 6(2) and 15(4). It seems likely that there has been an error in including para.16, which refers to investigations by the appropriate authority on its own behalf, and that what was intended was that reg.8 would not apply only in cases where the IPCC supervises, manages or conducts the investigation itself. This is the position in relation to the appointment of supervising officers: see reg.7.   2–077B

Regulation 10 of the Police (Conduct) Regulations 2004 provides that the investigating officer must submit his report: 2–079

- if the case concerns a senior officer, to the appropriate authority, or

- if the case did not concern a senior officer, to the supervising officer (it may be that, to satisfy para.22(2) of Sch.3 to the PRA, a copy would also have to be provided to the appropriate authority), and

- if the IPCC is supervising or managing the investigation, to the IPCC.

Acting on investigating officer's report

2–080   Similar duties to consider the possibility of a criminal offence being committed and to inform the Director of Public Prosecutions are imposed upon an appropriate authority undertaking an investigation on its own behalf: see the PRA, Sch.3, para.24(1)–(5).

2–083   Regulation 11 of the Police (Conduct) Regulations 2004 stipulates the steps to be taken by an appropriate authority in receipt of a report. In the case of a senior officer, the appropriate authority makes the decision whether or not to commence disciplinary proceedings; in other cases, the supervising officer does. (This may not be entirely consistent with the PRA: see Sch.3, para.24(6).) They have a general discretion whether or not to refer the case to a hearing, subject to an obligation to do so if certain conditions are met.

2–084A   The procedures for disciplinary hearings themselves are set out in regs 14 to 34 of the Police (Conduct) Regulations 2004 and the sanctions available to the tribunal are set out in reg.35. Under reg.29(2), the complainant or an interested person is entitled to attend the hearing up to and including the point at which the tribunal decides whether the conduct of the officer concerned met the appropriate standard. The complainant or interested person may request that questions be put to the officer concerned. If those questions might properly have been put by the officer presenting the case, they must be put to the officer, either by the tribunal or (at the tribunal's discretion) by the complainant or interested person: reg.29.

2–084B   There is no provision stipulating how the complainant should make his proposed questions known to the tribunal, which is master of its own procedure: reg.27. A complainant may wish to draft his questions beforehand, in which case it may be possible to hand them to the tribunal at the start of the hearing or at an appropriate moment after the presenting officer has cross-examined the officer concerned. But this is likely to be impracticable, since it will not be until the cross-examination has taken place that the complainant will know which additional questions are needed. It seems likely that the tribunal will have to allow the complainant a short period in which to consider his position and invite him to provide them with written or oral questions, the admissibility of which they can then decide upon.

Appeals by complainants

2–096   An appeal against a failure by a police authority or chief officer to determine who is the appropriate authority or to notify or record required details must be made within 28 days of the date on which notification of that failure is made or sent to the complainant: see Police (Complaints and Misconduct) Regulations 2004, reg.8(1). The IPCC may extend this time period under reg.8(8) where it is satisfied that in the special circumstances it is just to do so. The appeal must be in writing and contain:

- details of the complaint,

- the date on which the complaint is made,

- the name of the police force or police authority which gave notification of the failure,

- the grounds for the appeal,

- the date on which the complainant was notified of the failure.

The IPCC must then notify the police authority or chief officer (who must provide any information requested by the IPCC) and must determine the outcome of the appeal as soon as practicable: see reg.8. Similar provisions apply to appeals against local resolution decisions (reg.9) and appeals with respect to an investigation (reg.10).

    See para.2–083 above. The IPCC is empowered to present a disciplinary case   **2–098** at a tribunal by reg.25 of the Police (Conduct) Regulations 2004.

COMPLAINTS AND CIVIL ACTIONS

An officer against whom a recorded complaint is made is now entitled to a copy   **2–101** of it under reg.14 of the Police (Complaints and Misconduct) Regulations 2004, whether he is a senior officer or not and whether or not it leads to disciplinary proceedings, unless it might prejudice any criminal investigation or pending proceedings or would otherwise be contrary to the public interest. However, the copy may keep the identity of the complainant anonymous.

    The IPCC may dispense with a complaint if, among other things, it is not rea-   **2–105** sonably practicable to communicate with the complainant or a person acting on his behalf or it is not reasonably practicable to complete a satisfactory investigation in consequence of a refusal or failure on the part of the complainant to make a statement or afford other reasonable assistance or in consequence of the lapse of time: see the Police (Complaints and Misconduct) Regulations 2004, reg.3(2) and (4). The IPCC may also discontinue an investigation if the complainant refuses to co-operate to the extent that the IPCC considers that it is not reasonably practicable to continue with the investigation: reg.7. However, it is likely to be open to the IPCC to review any decision to dispense with a complaint or to discontinue an investigation if the circumstances change: see *R. (Wilkinson) v Police Complaints Authority and the Chief Constable of Merseyside Police* [2004] EWHC Admin 678.

CHAPTER 3

Practice and Procedure

BEGINNING AN ACTION

Initial Steps

Statements, photographs and other evidence

If the claimant has been examined by the Forensic Medical Examiner ("FME")   **3–018**
at the police station there will be two records which will be worth considering
before formulating a claim:

- The "Medical Register" completed at the police station—an extract from this is usually provided with the custody record (see *Civil Actions Against the Police* (3rd ed.), para.3–019).

- The FME's own clinical notes—a request for these should be made directly to the FME.

If the claimant has been taken to hospital after arrest a copy of the medical
notes should be obtained directly from the hospital. The contemporaneous
medical documents often record the claimant's own statements as to how the
injuries were caused and are important documents for the purposes of a
claim.

Actions in "warrant" cases

In *Bell v Chief Constable of Greater Manchester*, QBD, April 27, 2005,   **3–036**
para.105, Cooke J. held that no application having been made to set a warrant
aside it remained valid on its face and apt to protect the police by reason of s.6
of the Constable's Protection Act 1750.

Freedom of information

Introduction

The Freedom of Information Act 2000 ("FOIA") came into full force on January   **3–037A**
1, 2005. Police authorities and chief officers of police are "public authorities"

for the purposes of the FOIA (see FOIA, Sch.1, Pt V). Under s.1(1) of the FOIA, any person who requests information from a public authority is entitled (a) to be informed in writing by the public authority whether it holds information of the description specified in the request, and (b) if it does, to have that information communicated to him.

Requests, time limits and fees

3–037B   The FOIA states that "any person" may make a request. This includes natural persons, companies, statutory or other bodies, and unincorporated associations. There is no requirement of "standing"—anyone can make a request about anything. The person requesting the information does not have to reveal, much less justify, his reasons or motives for seeking the information. However, a public authority need not comply with a vexatious request or with repeated identical or substantially similar requests unless a reasonable period has elapsed since it complied with a previous request by the person in question.

3–037C   Section 84 of the FOIA defines "information" as "information recorded in any form". This clearly covers information recorded in documents as well as information recorded electronically, on tape or on video. In certain specific situations the FOIA provides that information includes unrecorded information.

3–037D   The public authority's duties to confirm or deny and to communicate apply to information held by it at the time when the request is received, subject to amendments or deletions which would have been made in the ordinary course of events regardless of the receipt of the request (s.1(4)). Information is held by a public authority if it is held by the authority or by another person on its behalf.

3–037E   The request for information must be in writing, must state the name of the applicant and his address, and must describe the information requested. It does not have to mention the FOIA. It may be transmitted by electronic means. Where the public authority reasonably requires further information in order to identify and locate the information requested, it may inform the applicant of that requirement whereupon it is not obliged to comply with its duty to confirm or deny or to communicate information until the applicant has supplied it with the further information it requires.

3–037F   The basic obligation of a public authority is to comply with its duties to confirm or deny and to communicate information "promptly and in any event not later than the 20th working day following the date of receipt" (s.10(1)). This tight timescale may be extended where the public authority reasonably requires further information from the applicant in order to identify and locate the information requested (s.1(3)).

3–037G   Under s.9, and subject to regulations on fees which may be made by the Secretary of State, it is open to a public authority to issue an applicant with a fees notice within the 20-day period following the request. Unless the fee demanded is paid within three months of the issue of the fee notice the public authority is not obliged to comply with its duties to confirm or deny or to communicate information. Public authorities can charge for photocopying and postage and will not charge for the costs of locating the information if this is less than £450 (on the basis of £25 per person hour). If the information costs public bodies more than £450 to produce they can either refuse to provide the information or require payment of the full cost.

Public authorities have a general duty under s.16 of the FOIA to provide advice and assistance to applicants for information. In discharging this duty they must have regard to the Code of Practice issued under s.45 which provides guidance on the discharge of functions under Pt I of FOIA.

3–037H

A separate Code of Practice has been issued under s.46 providing guidance on appropriate practices in connection with the keeping, management and destruction of records. Public authorities must also maintain publication schemes under s.19 which set out their policies with regard to the publication of different classes of information.

3–037I

Exemptions

There are three general categories of exemption: absolute exemptions, qualified exemptions and hybrid exemptions. The exemptions are formulated by reference to specified categories of information, but impact upon the duties to confirm or deny and to communicate information. There are six absolute exemptions (listed in s.2(3)), 15 qualified exemptions and three hybrid exemptions.

3–037J

The following "absolute" exemptions are potentially relevant to requests for information from the police:

3–037K

Section 21	information which is reasonably accessible to the applicant otherwise than under FOIA;
Section 23	information supplied by or relating to bodies dealing with security matters;
Section 32	court records;
Section 40:	Where the information constitutes personal data of which the applicant is the data subject (Note that this is a complex exemption which has some "qualified elements" and is therefore sometimes described as a "hybrid exemption).
Section 41	information obtained by a public authority from another person where disclosure of the information would constitute an actionable breach of confidence;
Section 44	disclosure prohibited by statute, Community obligation or court order.

If information falls within one of the absolute exemptions it is not subject to the right of access provided by FOIA. But, note that the reach of the absolute exemption under s.44 has been reduced significantly by delegated legislation introduced to repeal provisions in a number of statutes which would otherwise have prohibited the disclosure of information.

3–037L   The following "qualified exemptions" may be relevant to requests for information from the police:

Section 22	information intended for future publication;
Section 24	national security;
Section 26	defence;
Section 28	relations within the UK between the Government, the Scottish Administration, the Executive Committee of the Northern Ireland Assembly or the National Assembly for Wales;
Section 29	information prejudicial to the economic or financial interests of the UK;
Section 30	investigations and proceedings conducted by public authorities;
Section 31	information prejudicial to law enforcement;
Section 33	information prejudicial to audit functions;
Section 35	information relating to formulation of Government policy;
Section 38	information likely to endanger health or safety;
Section 39	environmental information;
Section 42	information in respect of which a claim for legal professional privilege could be maintained;
Section 43	trade secrets or information prejudicial to the commercial interests of any person.

3–037M   In the case of the "qualified exemptions" the exemption operates if either:

- in all the circumstances of the case the public interest in maintaining the exclusion of the duty to confirm or deny outweighs the public interest in disclosing whether the public authority holds the information; or

- in all the circumstances of the case the public interest in maintaining the exemption outweighs the public interest in disclosing the information.

3–037N   A public authority which considers that the information requested falls within a relevant exemption must, within 20 working days of the request, notify the applicant of its refusal, specifying the relevant exemption and stating (if not otherwise apparent) why the exemption applies (s.17(1)). Where the exemption on which the authority relies is not an absolute exemption and the authority has conducted the public interest balancing exercise referred to above, the authority must give reasons for its conclusion with or within a reasonable time of the notice of refusal.

FOIA requests in police cases

A large range of police documents which may be relevant to civil actions can now   3–037O
be obtained under the FOIA. These include documents such as the following:

- Policy documents—covering matters such as policies for the use of CS gas, stop and search and race equality.

- Documents concerning police staffing and administration.

- Documents concerning previous civil actions.

- Documents concerning particular police investigations.

It should, however, be noted that documents in the last category are likely to be subject to a number of exemptions. A number of police forces have made it clear that, in most cases, they seek to apply an exemption to prevent the release of information concerning investigations. Applications for information by a prospective claimant for information relating to him or herself will fall under the s.40 exemption but will be treated as a "subject access request" under the Data Protection Act 1998 (see *Civil Actions Against the Police* (3rd ed.), para.9–060).

STATEMENTS OF CASE

Reply

In a complex false imprisonment case it will be appropriate for the claimant to   3–053
serve a Reply so that the court can be clear about the factual issues between the parties. In *Austin v Commissioner of Police for the Metropolis* [2005] EWHC QB 480, para.26, Tugendhat J. said that a Reply should have been served "specifically admitting or denying the allegations in the Defences". He drew attention to the mandatory required for the service of a Reply in defamation actions where justification or fair comment is pleaded (CPR PD 53, para.2.8).

DISCLOSURE

Privilege and public interest immunity

Public interest immunity

The second ground for withholding the contents of an investigating officer's   3–064
disciplinary report as a "class claim" is further undermined by the new

provisions relating to the disclosure of such reports in the context of disciplinary proceedings: see para.23(12) of Sch.3 to the Police Reform Act 2002, para.2–026 above and *Civil Actions Against the Police* (3rd ed.), para.2–027. Note, however, that Sch.3, para.23(12) does not seek to remove "any obligation of secrecy imposed by any rule of law" other than in the context of disclosure of an investigating officer's report to a complainant.

TRIAL PROCEDURE

The claimant's case

Matters of evidence

3–113 **Similar fact evidence** The House of Lords upheld the decision of the Court of Appeal in *O'Brien v Chief Constable of South Wales* (see [2005] 1 W.L.R.1038) and took the opportunity to provide fresh guidance on the admissibility of similar fact evidence in civil cases. Lord Bingham explained the exercise to be undertaken in this way:

> "in a civil case. . . the question of admissibility turns, and turns only, on whether the evidence which it is sought to adduce, assuming it (provisionally) to be true, is in Lord Simon's sense, probative [that is, 'makes the matter which requires proof more or less probable']. If so, the evidence is legally admissible. That is the first stage of the enquiry.
>
> The second stage of the enquiry requires the case management judge or the trial judge to make what will often be a difficult and sometimes a finely balanced judgment: whether evidence or some of it (and if so which parts of it), which ex hypothesi is legally admissible, should be admitted." (paras 5 and 6)

Matters to be taken into account at the second stage include:

- the potential significance of the evidence in the context of the case as a whole;

- the degree to which it may distract the decision maker by focusing attention on collateral issues;

- its prejudicial value, weighed against its probative value—of special importance in a jury trial (see also para.55, *per* Lord Phillips);

- the administrative or costs burden which admission would lay on the resisting party;

- the lengthening of the trial;

- the fading of the recollections of witnesses.

The House of Lords thus confirmed that many matters which had previously been seen as rules limiting the admissibility of such evidence were in fact merely factors to be taken into account in a general balancing exercise undertaken by the trial judge at the second stage of the enquiry. There is no requirement to show enhanced or substantial probative value at the first stage of the enquiry— though the probative quality of the evidence may be relevant at the second stage (see paras 52 and 53). The fact that the evidence shows "mere propensity" does not necessarily preclude admission if it is relevant to the fact in issue (see para.73). Nor must the evidence necessarily be so similar to the matter in issue that coincidence can effectively be ruled out (para.77).

Obtaining a verdict from the jury

The role of the jury in determining liability

This passage from *Dallison v Caffery* was cited once again with approval by the Court of Appeal in *Larrier v Chief Constable of Merseyside Police* [2004] EWCA Civ 246 at [23]–[24]. The principles were summarised as follows: **3–124**

> "It is for the judge to decide whether there is sufficient evidence to go to the jury on any particular issue and to adjudicate upon the reasonableness of the actions of police officers. However, where there is a conflict of evidence between the parties on a relevant issue of fact, it is for the jury to decide that issue."

Jury questions in false imprisonment cases

The jury may also need to decide whether the police officer's discretion to arrest was exercised in good faith, which may go beyond whether the officer had an honest suspicion or belief that the claimant was guilty of an offence. In *Paul v Chief Constable of Humberside Police* [2004] EWCA Civ 308, Brooke L.J. said that: **3–129**

> "there was evidence to go to the jury in this case in the issue of the police's good faith in deciding to arrest Mr Paul rather than to permit him to help them voluntarily, and the judge should not have withdrawn this issue from the jury. He would have had to direct them to consider this question unless, as I have said, he had ruled that there was no evidence to support Mr Paul's case on this point." (at [37])

Jury questions in malicious prosecution cases

3–133   It was reiterated in *McHarg v Chief Constable of Thames Valley Police* [2004] EWHC QB 5 that (i) if there is no evidence more consistent with malice than the absence of malice, there is no evidence of malice to go to the jury ([22]) and (ii) the honesty of a prosecutor's belief in reasonable and probable cause should only be left to the jury if there is some affirmative evidence of lack of honest belief ([25]).

Jury questions in negligence cases

3–138A   As with assault, a claim in negligence which would usually be tried by judge alone can come before a jury because it has been brought together with a claim for false imprisonment or malicious prosecution. In *Hutt v Commissioner of Police for the Metropolis* [2003] EWCA Civ 1911, the Court of Appeal considered the proper approach in such a case. Hale LJ said that:

> "Negligence is a mixed question of fact and law. It is very difficult to pick apart. The judge had two options. First, even if the case involved false imprisonment so that the claimant had a right to demand a jury trial under section 69(1) of the Supreme Court Act or section 66(3) of the County Courts Act, the court could use its general case management powers under CPR Part 31.1(2) to deal separately with different allegations in the same action. Secondly, if he decided to involve the jury he should retain the usual separation functions, ask the jury some specific questions and decide whether the answers to those questions amounted to negligence in fact." (at [27])

The existence of a duty of care is a matter of law for the judge, though there may well be factual issues underlying it, but whether reasonable care was taken is a matter of fact for the jury (see *Civil Actions Against the Police* (3rd ed.), para.8–013). It suggested that Hale L.J. was contemplating simply that the factual elements of negligence (breach of duty, causation, and damage) be left to the jury by means of specific questions, the legal questions (duty of care and certain elements of recoverability of damage) be decided by the judge, and then the judge consider the full picture in determining whether negligence has been made out.

CHAPTER 4

Intentional Torts to the Person

FALSE IMPRISONMENT

Definition

4-034   In *R. v Governor of Brockhill Prison Ex p. Evans (No.2)* [2001] 2 A.C. 19, (43F), Lord Hobhouse emphasised the fact that the tort of false imprisonment is a constitutional safeguard of the liberty of the subject against the executive. In *A v Secretary of State for the Home Office* [2005] 2 W.L.R. 87, para.79, Lord Hope said that "It is impossible ever to overstate the importance of the right to liberty in a democracy".

The nature and character of the defendant's act

4-036A   The nature of the "restraint of movement" required for the tort of false imprisonment appears to be different from that required for there to be a "deprivation of liberty" for the purposes of Art.5 (see *Austin v Commissioner of Police for the Metropolis* [2005] EWHC QB 480, at [45]).

4-037   n.5: The Court of Human Rights found that the detention of the claimant in *Re L* was a breach of Art.5: see *HL v United Kingdom* (Judgment of October 5, 2004).

4-038   n.6: However, there may be a false imprisonment if the notional means of escape is unreasonable—as, for instance, involving risk to life or limb: see *Burton v Davies and Anor* [1953] Q.S.R. 26, particularly at 30, *per* Townley J.

     n.7: See also *Watson v Marshall* (1971) 124 C.L.R. 621, 626, *per* Walsh J.

The liability of a third party for an arrest by a police officer

4-046   The Ontario Supreme Court of Justice has held that a person will be "responsible" for an arrest if he was "actively instrumental in the decision to arrest and detain" (*Tschekalin and others v Brunette and others* [2004] O.J. 2855, para.70). In *Hanisch v Canada* [2004] B.C.D. Civ. J. 3249, at [30]), the British Columbia Court of Appeal that the question was whether the defendant:

> "went beyond laying information before police officers for them to take such action as they thought fit and amounted to some direction, or procuring, or direct request, or direct encouragement that they should act by way of arresting [the claimant]".

GENERAL DEFENCES TO TRESPASS TO THE PERSON

Introduction

Where claimant seeks to rebut a defence of lawful detention on "public law"   4-069
grounds it is not an abuse of the process to bring a private law action for damages for false imprisonment in the county court (see *ID v Home Office* [2005]
EWCA Civ 38).

n.87: See also *Youssef v Home Office* [2004] EWHC QB 1884.

Self-defence and related purposes

In *Ashley v Chief Constable of Sussex Police* [2005] EWHC QB 415, at [42],   4-077
Dobbs J. took the view that it was for a claimant to show that force used against
him was *not* in self-defence because "there has to be an application of 'unlawful' force in order for the allegation [of assault] to be made out". It is suggested
that this is incorrect for the reasons given in *Civil Actions Against the Police*
(3rd ed.), para.4-006 ff. Any intentional application of force to another is a trespass to the person unless it falls within what is generally accepted in the ordinary conduct of everyday life. Self-defence is a defence to a trespass to the
person which, it is suggested, has to be proved by the defendant: see *Dallison v
Caffery* [1965] 1 Q.B. 348 at 365; *Paul v Chief Constable of Humberside Police*
[2004] EWCA Civ 308, at [30] and see also the comments of May L.J. in
R (Laporte) v Chief Constable of Gloucestershire Constabulary [2004] 2 All
E.R. 874, para.113 and *Clerk & Lindsell on Torts* (18th ed.), para.13–37.

Necessity

In *Austin v Commissioner of Police for the Metropolis* [2005] EWHC QB 480,   4-085
at [574ff], Tugendhat J. held that the purposes for the imposition of an
"absolute cordon" around a crowd in Oxford Circus in London on May 1, 2001
the prevention of serious injury and possible death and to protect property and
that, as a result, there was a defence of necessity to the false imprisonment
claim of members of the crowd.

n.33: See also the discussion of necessity in *R v Bournewood Mental Health
Trust, Ex. p. L* [1999] 1 A.C. 458, 488–490, *per* Lord Goff.

Preventing a breach of the peace

4–089   The Court of Appeal took a less strict approach to anticipated breaches of the peace in *R. (Laporte) v Chief Constable of Gloucestershire Constabulary* [2005] 1 All E.R. 473, in which it was held that it was lawful for the police to refuse to allow a coach party to travel to Fairford air base to protest against the war in Iraq when it was suspected some of that party intended to cause violence there. The Court said that:

> "We regard what is sufficiently 'imminent' to justify taking action to prevent a breach of the peace as dependent on all the circumstances. As in *Moss's* case, it is important that the claimant was intending to travel in a vehicle if the preventative action had not taken place. The relatively small distance involved [less than 5km by road and 2km by foot] did not mean there was no sufficient imminence. What preventive action was necessary and proportionate, however, would be very much influenced by how close in proximity, both in place and time, the location of the apprehended breach of the peace was. The greater the distance and the greater the time involved, the more important it is to decide whether preventive action is really necessary and, if it is necessary, the more restrained the action taken should usually be as there will be time for further action if the action initially taken does not deter. It may be that as the police thought, arrest at the lay-by would have been a disproportionate level of action, but this does not necessarily mean that no action was appropriate." (para.44)

Thus, on the facts of that case, it was lawful to prevent the coach from travelling to Fairford. However, escorting the coach back to London and refusing to allow it to leave the motorway for the two-and-a-half hour journey was disproportionate and unreasonable, and therefore unlawful.

4–089A   It appears from *Laporte* that a measure affecting one person may be lawful if necessary to prevent a breach of the peace being committed *by another person* if it is not possible to distinguish which members of a group pose the threat. The Court said that:

> "In view of the attitude adopted generally by the occupants of the coaches, it is difficult to see how it would be possible to distinguish between the occupants. . . The important point to note about the ability to take preventative action is that its justification is not derived from the person against whom the action is taken having actually committed an offence, but based upon the need to *prevent* the apprehended breach of the peace. In some situations, preventing a breach of the peace will only be possible if action is taken which risks affecting a wholly innocent individual." (para.48)

It may be arguable that this apparent extension of the law was *obiter* because, on the one hand, no tort would have been committed in any event by preventing the coach from travelling to Fairford: this did not amount to a detention for the purposes of false imprisonment or Art.5 of the Convention (see para.51). On the other hand, the *actual* detention (that is, the enforced journey to London with the passengers confined to the coach) was held unlawful because it was disproportionate and unreasonable. The fact that there was a group of people was therefore decisive for neither point. Nevertheless, the court made clear that there may be circumstances where such detention of a group of people *would* have been lawful (para.54).

A similar situation arose in *Austin v Commissioner of Police for the Metropolis* [2005] EWHC QB 480, in which Tugendhat J. held that the detention of a large group of people in Oxford Circus in London on May Day 2001 for several hours was lawful. This was unquestionably a "detention" for the purposes of the common law. However, Tugendhat J. appeared to take the view that the containment of the group was only lawful because the police reasonably and honestly believed that *each* of those present were about to commit a breach of the peace. Tugendhat J. applied a test analogous to s.24 of PACE, holding that:

4–089B

> "the test for deciding whether a measure short of arrest can be lawfully taken against a given individual should also be reasonable suspicion that that individual is presenting the relevant threat. I take this to mean the same thing as 'reasonably appear' and the other expressions used in the cases. So when the police reasonably consider it necessary to prevent someone in a group from committing an offence, that someone may be anyone whom the officer reasonably suspects to be about to commit the offence." ([52])

He concluded that:

> "subject to personal matters which might have arisen for consideration when each Claimant came forward and asked to be released, it did appear to the police (that is the police did suspect) that all those present within the cordon, including each Claimant, were demonstrators, and that in the particular circumstances of this case, that meant that they also appeared to the police to be about to commit that breach of the peace." ([529]).

It may be that the Court of Appeal in *Laporte* was saying the same thing in different language: if the police suspect that some people in a group pose a threat of violence, but are truly unable to detect which particular individuals pose the threat, it may be said that they suspect each member of that group to pose that threat unless and until they gain information which enables them to make distinctions. Tugendhat J. suggested that a similar conclusion "is unlikely to be capable of being drawn in all crowd cases" ([530])—suggesting that such an argument is only likely to be accepted in limited circumstances.

4–090   See also *Steel v UK* (1998) 28 E.H.R.R. 603, for the understanding of the European Court of Human Rights that:

> "the concept of breach of peace has been clarified by the English courts over the last two decades, to the extent that it is now sufficiently established that a breach of the peace is committed only when an individual causes harm, or appears likely to cause harm, to persons or property or acts in a manner the natural consequences of which would be to provoke others to violence."

CHAPTER 5

Police Powers over the Person: Arrest, Detention and other Miscellaneous Powers

INTRODUCTION

5–002A   The burden of establishing that an assault, battery or false imprisonment is lawful is on the police (see *Civil Actions Against the Police* (3rd ed.), para.4–069). If, however, the claimant is challenging the lawfulness of the exercise of a discretionary power to interfere with his person or liberty the burden is on him/her to show that the discretion was exercised unlawfully (see Supplement, para.5–060, below). It is not clear whether, when the claimant challenges the exercise of a discretion, the *Wednesbury* test should be applied or whether, because fundamental rights are in play, the court is the primary decision maker (see Supplement, para.5–080, below). A measure taken by the police to arrest or detain a person will not be lawful if it breaches any of the person's rights under the European Convention on Human Rights (see *Austin v Commissioner of Police for the Metropolis* [2005] EWHC QB 480, at [40]).

DETENTION SHORT OF ARREST, STOP AND SEARCH

Common law powers of detention short of arrest

It has been suggested that the police have a common law power of temporary   5–003A
detention, short of arrest, for so long as is necessary to protect the rights of others and is consistent with public safety (see *Austin v Commissioner of Police for
the Metropolis* [2005] EWHC QB 480, at [40]). It was said that the test for
deciding whether a measure short of arrest can be lawfully taken against an
individual is whether there is "reasonable suspicion" that the individual is
presenting the relevant threat (para.152).

The statutory powers to stop and search

The general power under PACE

n.16: From July 1, 2005, it will also include prohibited fireworks: see s.115 of the   5–007
Serious Organised Crime and Police Act 2005 and para.3 of the Serious
Organised Crime and Police Act 2005 (Commencement No.1, Transitional and
Transitory Provisions) Order 2005 (SI 2005/1521).

Other statutory stop and search powers

The scope of the stop and search powers under the Terrorism Act 2000 was con-   5–023
sidered by the Court of Appeal in *R. (Gillan) v Commissioner of Police for the
Metropolis* [2005] Q.B. 388.

    There is a new statutory power short of arrest under s.112 of the Serious   5–023A
Organised Crime and Police Act 2005, which will come into force on July 1,
2005 (see para.3 of the Serious Organised Crime and Police Act 2005
(Commencement No.1, Transitional and Transitory Provisions) Order 2005 (SI
2005/1521)). This will allow a constable to direct a person to leave a place if he
believes, on reasonable grounds, that the person would be prohibited from
entering that place as a result of:

(a) an order made by virtue of an enactment following the person's
conviction for an offence;

(b) a condition imposed by virtue of a person's release from prison in which
he was serving a sentence of imprisonment following conviction of an
offence;

(c)   an order or condition prohibiting the person from entering the place.

The direction can be given orally.

Stop and search and the European Convention on Human Rights

5–026   In *R. (Gillan) v Commissioner of Police for the Metropolis* [2005] Q.B. 388, the Court of Appeal considered the lawfulness of the stop and search powers under ss.44 and 45 of the Terrorism Act 2000 which, like those under s.60 of the Criminal Justice and Public Order Act 1994, require general authorisation from a chief officer but do not require any reasonable suspicion on the part of the constable involved in relation to the individuals stopped, were lawful. It seems likely that a similar approach would be taken to s.60.

5–026A   The court held that the provisions of the statute did not themselves conflict with the European Convention on Human Rights, but the exercise of the powers thereby conferred might be incompatible with the Convention (para.32). The court took the view that the use of stop and search powers probably would not constitute a deprivation of liberty so as to engage Art.5, at least if the detention was short (paras 45–56). However, it accepted that Art.8 (the right to privacy) was engaged by stops and searches (para.47). It was held that any interference with the rights under either Article was capable of being justified in order to "secure the fulfilment of any objective prescribed by law", namely the prevention and deterrence of terrorist attack (para.44). However, the police have to satisfy the court that the exercise of the powers was proportionate to *and* in genuine pursuance of that aim (although the court will pay due regard to the view of the executive authorities—paras 33–35). Because of the unsatisfactory evidence before the Court, the Commissioner had not proved that the powers under the Terrorism Act were in fact used at an "operational" level for the lawful purpose of preventing terrorism, as opposed to the unlawful purposes of policing a demonstration against an arms fair in London (para.56). Accordingly, the stops and searches were unlawful. An appeal is pending before the House of Lords.

ARREST: DEFINITION AND REASONS AND PROCEDURE

The obligation to give reasons for an arrest

Common law and s.28 of PACE

5–036   In *Taylor v Chief Constable of Thames Valley Police* [2004] 1 W.L.R. 3155, the Court of Appeal reviewed the authorities and held that:

"the modern approach to the application of section 28(3) is that set out in para 40 of the judgment in *Fox, Campbell and Hartley v United Kingdom* 13 EHRR 157, 170. The question is thus whether, having regard to all the circumstances of the particular case, the person arrested was told in simple, non-technical language that he could understand, the essential legal and factual grounds for his arrest. In light of the case law as it has developed, I doubt whether it will in the future be necessary to consider the cases in any detail, or perhaps at all. It seems to me that in the vast majority of cases it will be sufficient to ask the question posed by the European Court of Human Rights." (para.26)

The question is objective, but the position of the arrested person is relevant: it may not always be reasonable to expect a child to understand language which an adult could reasonably be expected to understand (paras 59–60). However, whether the claimant does *in fact* understand is irrelevant (though this does not, of course, prevent the *expression* of a lack of understanding being relevant). On the facts of the case it was sufficient to tell a 10-year old claimant that he was being arrested for violent disorder at a particular place on a particular date.

ARREST WITHOUT WARRANT I: ARRESTABLE OFFENCES AND REASONABLE GROUNDS

Introduction

Section 110 of the Serious Organised Crime and Police Act 2005 ("SOCPA") will make radical changes to the powers of arrest contained in PACE. The existing powers of arrest in ss.24 and 25 will be replaced and extended. The new police powers of arrest will be contained in a new s.24; the new powers of arrest open to all members of the public will be contained in a new s.24A. Section 25 will be repealed. Section 110 of SOCPA will come into force on a date to be appointed by the Secretary of State (see s.178 of SOCPA).

5–049A

Powers of arrest under SOCPA

Police powers of arrest

Under the new provisions police officers will gain a new, overarching power of arrest in relation to *any* offence. Two broad requirements will need to be satisfied. The first requirement spans new s.24(1), (2) and (3) and relates to the relationship between the suspect and the offence. Broadly, it will be satisfied if the suspect has committed, is committing, or is about to commit an offence *or* if the

5–049B

police officer has reasonable grounds to suspect that the suspect has committed, is committing, or is about to commit an offence. The second requirement is found in new s.24(4) and (5) and relates to the necessity of effecting the arrest. The officer must have "reasonable grounds for believing that . . . it is necessary to arrest the person in question" for one of the following reasons:

(a) to enable the name of the person in question to be ascertained;

(b) to enable the address of the person in question to be ascertained;

(c) to prevent the person in question—

    (i) causing physical injury to himself or any other person;
    (ii) suffering physical injury;
    (iii) causing loss or damage to property;
    (iv) committing an offence against public decency—where members of the public going about their normal business cannot reasonably be expected to avoid the person;
    (v) causing an unlawful obstruction of the highway.

(d) to protect a child or other vulnerable person from the person in question;

(e) to allow prompt and effective investigation of the offence or of the conduct of the person in question; or

(f) to prevent the prosecution of the offence from being hindered by the disappearance of the person in question.

5–049C   The main result of this will be to remove the concept of "arrestable offences" now contained in s.24 of PACE (see para.24 of Sch. 7 to SOCPA) and to expand what are currently known as the "general arrest conditions" by adding the new potential reasons for arrest in s.24(5)(e) and (f) above. These are very broadly worded. At present, broadly speaking, arrests on suspicion of minor offences can only be made when identification is in issue, to prevent crime, or for the protection of the suspect or others. In future, they will be able to be made for the purposes of furthering the investigation or to prevent the suspect disappearing. This is a major extension to the current powers and has attracted concern (see, for example, *Liberty's Briefing for the Second Reading in the House of Commons* (December 2004)).

5–049D   In terms of the approach which the courts are likely to take when considering the lawfulness of arrests under the new provisions, there is no reason to think that the first requirement will lead to any changes: the police will still need to show an honest suspicion of the suspect's guilt on reasonable grounds or show that an offence was or was being or was going to be committed by the suspect (see *Civil Actions Against the Police* (3rd ed.), para.5–060ff). However, the second requirement will require a new approach. The police will also have to show an honest belief in and reasonable grounds for believing in the *necessity of the arrest* for one of the reasons listed in new s.24(5). This in effect circumscribes the "discretion" a police officer currently has to arrest. It is suggested that it is likely that it will now be easier to challenge this element of the decision to arrest, which is probably currently challengeable only on *Wednesbury* unreasonableness grounds or on the *Wednesbury*-plus approach suggested in *Al-Fayed v Commissioner of Police for the Metropolis* [2004] EWCA Civ 1579 (see generally Supplement, para.5–086, below).

There are three reasons for this:

- the court will be able to scrutinise the decision more closely: the wording of the legislation makes it clear that *Wednesbury* unreasonableness will no longer be appropriate;

- it is submitted that, in accordance with the approach to the lawfulness of an arrest for an arrestable offence (see *Civil Actions Against the Police* (3rd ed.), para.5–060) the burden is on the police to show that the arresting officer has honestly and reasonably believed in the necessity of the arrest;

- the grounds relied on must support not just "suspicion" but "belief", which requires a higher level of persuasion (see *Civil Actions Against the Police* (3rd ed.), paras 5–088—5–090).

Moreover, if the reason relied upon is identification, then the officer will also have to show why the arrest was necessary in light of the new power to take fingerprint and other identification evidence at the roadside under s.117 of SOCPA.

The idea behind the new provisions was, apparently, to simplify the 5–049E arrest process (see the Home Office consultation: *Policing: Modernising Police Powers to Meet Community Needs*, which can be found at *www.homeoffice.gov.uk/docs3/policingconsultation.pdf*, para.2). It must be questionable whether s.110 of SOCPA achieves this. The result is, on the one hand, to seriously enlarge the circumstances under which a person may be arrested and, on the other, to require police officers to undertake a nuanced exercise and decide whether arrest (now with no guidance on which offences are "arrestable" or "serious") is "necessary" for a number of specific reasons, which can be examined closely by the courts. In truth, however, it must be questionable whether the court's higher scrutiny of those judgments will fully balance the substantial extension of the power to arrest because the grounds available to be police are so broadly worded. The result may well be more arrests.

Several police powers—such as searches, extended detention, and the ability 5–049F to set up road checks—are dependent on an arrest for or a suspicion of the commission of a "serious arrestable offence". This concept will disappear when para.43(12) of Sch.7 to SOCPA comes into force; it will be replaced in most cases by the much lower threshold of an "indictable offence". Many of the particular provisions affected are highlighted below where they appear in *Civil Actions Against the Police* (3rd ed.).

Arrest by persons other than police officers

5–049G   A similar two-stage process will also apply to arrests made by persons other than police officers, which will be governed by new s.24A. any person may arrest without a warrant:

(a)   anyone who is in the act of committing an indictable offence;

(b)   anyone whom he has reasonable grounds for suspecting to be committing an indictable offence;

(c)   any person who is guilty of committing an indictable offence; or

(d)   any person whom he has reasonable grounds for suspecting to be guilty of committing an indictable offence, provided that offence has, in fact, been committed by someone.

5–049H   There is also the need for "necessity". Two requirements must both be satisfied:

(1)   the person making the arrest must have reasonable grounds for believing it is necessary to arrest the person in questions for any of the following reasons:

(a)   to prevent the person in question injuring himself or any other person;
(b)   to prevent the person in question suffering physical injury;
(c)   to prevent the person in question causing loss of or damage to property; or
(d)   to prevent the person in question making off before a constable can assume responsibility for him; **and**

(2)   it must appear to the person making the arrest that it is not reasonably practicable for a constable to make it instead.

As previously, therefore, the powers of arrest accorded to normal persons are more circumscribed than those available to the police. There *is* a seriousness threshold here: the offence must be an indictable offence. Further, a person will only be entitled to make an arrest for an offence he believes to have been committed in the past if it has in fact been committed by someone; a police officer need only have a reasonable suspicion of the past commission of the offence. Clearly, the potential justifications for arrest are also much more limited.

The lawfulness of an arrest for an arrestable offence

Introduction

The statement in *Civil Actions Against the Police* (3rd ed.) that the burden of   5–060
proving that the discretion to arrest has been exercised improperly is on the
claimant was approved in *Austin v Commissioner of Police for the Metropolis*
[2005] EWHC QB 480, paras 157–161, citing *Al Fayed v Commissioner of
Police for the Metropolis* [2004] EWCA Civ 1579, at [83].

The subjective question: the suspicion

It may not be necessary for an arresting officer to have a particular offence in   5–061
mind, if he honestly and reasonably suspects the claimant to be guilty of conduct which would give rise to a number of offences: *Coudrat v Commissioners
of Customs & Excise* [2005] EWCA Civ 616, at [32].

The objective question: reasonable grounds

In *Cumming v Chief Constable of Northumbria Police* [2003] EWCA Civ 1844,   5–064
the Court of Appeal reiterated that suspicion alone is not sufficient render an
arrest lawful: the "objective" test must still be satisfied and so the court still
needs to determine whether or not the police had facts or information to support the suspicion (see [12] and [37]). Latham L.J. approved a comment made
by Sir Frederick Lawton in *Castorina v Chief Constable of Surrey* [1996] L.G.
Rev. Rep.241 that:

> "Suspicion by itself, however, will not justify an arrest. There must be a fac-
> tual basis for it of a kind which the court would adjudge to be reasonable."

The case of *Cumming v Chief Constable of Northumbria Police* [2003]   5–071
EWCA Civ 1844, provides a further example of the limited burden of proving
reasonable grounds. In that case, the claimants were employed by the South
Tyneside Metropolitan Borough Council to monitor CCTV cameras. A col-
league of theirs noticed a young man apparently attempting to steal a car. The
young man was arrested but, when the police came to view the CCTV footage,
the tapes appeared to have been tampered with. Some weeks later, the Council
had narrowed the potential culprits to six, including the claimants. The police
arrested them all. The Court of Appeal held that the arrests were lawful,
Latham LJ holding that:

> "there is nothing in principle which prevents opportunity from amounting to
> reasonable grounds for suspicion . . . Again, there can be nothing in principle

wrong with arresting more than one person even if the crime can only have been committed by one person . . . Where a small number of people can be clearly identified as the only ones capable of having committed the offence, I see no reason why that cannot afford reasonable grounds for suspecting each of them . . .". [31]

Brooke L.J. expressed his unease at the outcome and expressly limited the case to its particular facts, including the fact that the police believed that the employer had carried out a full and proper investigation which had yielded no information from the claimants ([46]–[48]).

5–081   In *Clements v DPP* [2005] EWHC Admin 1279, the Divisional Court reached the surprising conclusion that the fact that a person was a young man was a matter which could properly be taken into account in determining whether a police officer had reasonable grounds to suspect that he was likely to damage to property in an anti-war demonstration.

The discretion to make an arrest

5–085   The Court of Appeal has recently reiterated that it may be a proper exercise of discretion to arrest a person solely in order to assert maximum pressure to obtain a confession: see *Cumming v Chief Constable of Northumbria Police* [2003] EWCA Civ 1844, [42]–[44].

In *Paul v Chief Constable of Humberside Police* [2004] EWCA Civ 308, at

5–086   [30], Brooke L.J. summarised the position in relation to the discretion to arrest in the following terms:

"Section 24(6) of the Police and Criminal Evidence Act ('PACE') 1984 created a power or discretion, not a duty, to arrest, and this discretion is subject to judicial control (see *Hussein v Chong Fook Kam* [1970] AC 942, 948). This judicial control is exercised on conventional administrative law principles (*Mohammed-Holgate v Duke* [1984] AC 437, 443; *Cumming v Chief Constable of Northumbria Police* [2003] EWCA Civ 1844 at [43]—[44]). The discretion is that of the individual arresting officer (*O'Hara v Chief Constable of the Royal Ulster Constabulary* [1987] AC 286). It must be exercised in good faith (*Mohammed-Holgate* at 443). In *Cumming* Latham LJ observed at para 44 that although Article 5 of the European Convention of Human Rights does not require the court to evaluate the exercise of discretion in any different way as it evaluates the exercise of any other executive discretion, it must do so in the light of the important right to liberty which is at stake".

The comments on the test to be applied were *obiter*. The point arose for decision in *Youssef v Home Office* [2004] EWHC QB 1884. Field J. held that the reasonableness of the Home Secretary's view that there was a real prospect of being able to remove the claimant to Egypt in compliance with Art.3 of the Convention had to be judged by the court as primary decision-maker rather than on the *Wednesbury* standard. This decision was mentioned by Brooke L.J. in *ID v Home Office* [2005] EWCA Civ 38, [102], without discussion of the point (see also, [107]). In *Al Fayed v Commissioner of Police for the Metropolis* [2004] EWCA Civ 1579, at [83(4)], Auld L.J. expressed the view that the "generous ambit" of *Wednesbury* discretion may be narrowed by human rights jurisprudence and, the more substantial the inference with the right to liberty, the narrower the otherwise generous *Wednesbury* ambit of reasonableness becomes. This is described as *Wednesbury*-plus reasonableness ([82]). In *Austin v Commissioner of Police for the Metropolis* [2005] EWHC QB 480, at [166]) Tugendhat J. concluded that the Court should have a high degree of respect for the executive decisions of police officers who decide to arrest suspects.

ARREST WITHOUT WARRANT II: GENERAL POWERS OF ARREST, ARREST FOR FINGERPRINTING AND OTHER STATUTORY POWERS

General powers of arrest

Section 25 of PACE will be revoked and replaced with new powers under new ss.24 and 24A when s.110 of the Serious Organised Crime and Police Act 2005 comes into force on a date to be appointed: see Supplement, para.5–048, above.

5–094

THE DETENTION OF SUSPECTS IN POLICE CUSTODY

The custody officer

Sections 120 and 121 of the Serious Organised Crime and Police Act 2005 will allow most of the duties of custody officers to be undertaken by civilian staff designated to the role of "staff custody officers". The provisions come into force on a date to be appointed by the Secretary of State under s.178 of the Act. There are at least two views on the wisdom of this move. On the one hand, it may lead to more independent custody officers and help to alleviate some of the concerns raised about the present system (see, for example, *Civil Actions Against the Police* (3rd ed.), paras I–012 and 5–144). On the other, it may be more difficult for civilian staff to question the conduct of police officers bringing an arrested person before them.

5–128

The power to detain, charge and release

The custody officer's duty when the suspect is charged

5–138   The Court of Appeal confirmed in *Hutt v Commissioner of Police for the Metropolis* [2003] EWCA Civ 1911, at [16]–[19], that the custody officer's powers under s.38(1) of PACE to detain a suspect after charge are contingent on a prior, lawful arrest.

The custody officer's duty where there is insufficient evidence to charge

5–145   The test in *Wilding v Chief Constable of Lancashire* was cited with apparent approval by the Court of Appeal in *Taylor v Chief Constable of Thames Valley Police* [2004] 1 W.L.R. 3155, paras 45, and in *Al-Fayed v Commissioner of Police for the Metropolis* [2004] EWCA Civ 1579, at [96ff]. In neither case did the court consider the points dealt with in *Civil Actions Against the Police* (3rd ed.).

5–145A   In *Coudrat v Commissioners of Her Majesty's Customs & Excise* [2005] EWCA Civ 616, at [37], the trial judge had failed to deal with the question as to whether detention is "necessary" to secure, preserve or obtain evidence at all. However, the Court of Appeal upheld his finding that the continued detention was lawful on the basis that there were reasonable grounds for the arrest and "the custody officer would have known that the customs officers wanted to interview the appellant for the purposes of finding further evidence against him if they could". The custody officer had not even been called to give evidence (though it appears that this was because it was not clear until the trial itself that the lawfulness of the *continued* detention was in issue). It is submitted that this is the wrong approach and, in the absence of proper evidence justifying the continuing detention it should have been held to have been unlawful.

The power to authorise continued detention

5–165   When para.43(7) of Sch.3 to the Serious Organised Crime and Police Act 2005 comes into force on a date to be appointed by the Secretary of State, continued detention will be available where the suspect is suspected of an indictable offence. The concept of a "serious arrestable offence" will disappear from PACE (see para. 5–048, above).

The power to apply for further detention

5–173   When para.43(8) of Sch.3 to the Serious Organised Crime and Police Act 2005 comes into force on a date to be appointed by the Secretary of State, s.43 of

PACE will be amended so that a magistrate can issue a warrant of further detention where the suspect is arrested for an indictable offence rather than a serious arrestable offence. The concept of a "serious arrestable offence" will disappear from PACE (see para.5–048 above).

SEARCH, SAMPLES AND FINGERPRINTING

Fingerprinting

Section 117 of the Serious Organised Crime and Police Act 2005 will insert a new sub-section (6A) into s.61 of PACE, allowing a constable to take fingerprints from a person where:
    5–207

(a) he reasonably suspects that the person is committing or attempting to commit an offence, or has committed or attempted to commit an offence; and

(b) the name of the person is unknown to, and cannot be readily ascertained by, the constable or the constable has reasonable grounds for doubting whether a name furnished by the person as his name is his real name.

If these conditions are met, fingerprints may be taken at place other than a police station. However, fingerprints taken under s.61(6A) must be destroyed as soon as they have fulfilled the purpose for which they were taken. These powers will come into force on a date to be appointed by the Secretary of State (s.178 of the 2005 Act).

Footwear and photographs

Section 118 of the Serious Organised Crime and Police Act 2005 will insert into PACE provisions relating to the taking of footwear impressions which are similar to the existing provisions relating to the taking of fingerprints. The date on which these provisions will come into force will be appointed by the Secretary of State.
    5–210A

There are also new provisions related to photographing, extending those under s.64A of PACE. When s.116 of SOCPA is brought into force "photograph" will include "moving images", for example. However, perhaps the most important new power will be the power to photograph a person outside a police station in certain circumstances.
    5–210B

Intimate samples

5–211   Section 119(2) of the Serious Organised Crime and Police Act 2005 expands the definition of "intimate sample" to include "a swab taken from any part of a person's genitals (including the pubic hair)". This section will come into force on July 1, 2005 by virtue of para.3 of the Serious Organised Crime and Police Act 2005 (Commencement No.1, Transitional and Transitory Provisions) Order 2005 (SI 2005/1521).

Non-intimate samples

5–214   To reflect the new definition of "intimate sample" (see Supplement, para.5–211, above), from July 1, 2005, any swab taken from a person's body which would not be an intimate sample will be a "non-intimate sample": see s.119(3) of the Serious Organised Crime and Police Act 2005. This means any swab, except one taken from a body orifice other than the mouth or one taken from any part of a person's genitals (including the pubic hair), will be a "non-intimate sample".

Searches, samples, fingerprints and the European Convention on Human Rights

5–221   In *R. (Marper) v Chief Constable of South Yorkshire Police* [2004] 1 W.L.R. 2196), the House of Lords took the view that, while the *taking* of fingerprints and samples clearly interfered with a person's private life within the meaning of Art.8(1), the *retention* of those fingerprints did not, and that any interference was objectively justified in any event (see paras 21, 31, 40 and 41). The case of *Rotaru v Romania* (2000) 8 B.H.R.C. 449 (see *Civil Actions Against the Police* (3rd ed.), para.9–036)—which establishes that the compilation of data by the state engages Art.8—does not appear to have been cited. The House of Lords held that it was not unlawfully discriminatory to retain samples taken lawfully from innocent persons in the course of a criminal investigation when the police had no samples in relation to the public at large (see paras 42–56).

CHAPTER 6

Interfering with Land and Goods

TRESPASS TO LAND: DEFENCES

Consent or "licence"

Implied licences

6–040   It was pointed out by the New Zealand Court of Appeal in *R v Bradley* (1997) 15 C.R.N.Z. 363, 368 that:

> "the scope of the implied permission for a police officer to pursue his or her legitimate business will not necessarily be the same as the implied licence of, say, a postman or stranger merely seeking directions. The lawful business of each differs, and with that difference, the occupier's expectation of privacy may also differ. The scope of the authority to enter may vary so as to permit that which, having regard to the householder's reasonable expectation of privacy, is reasonable in the circumstances".

Necessity

6–047   In *Dehn v A-G* [1988] 2 N.Z.L.R. 564, 580, it was held that the "necessity principle" permitted entry where a person:

> "believes in good faith and upon grounds which are objectively reasonable that it is necessary to do so in order (1) to preserve human life, or (2) to prevent serious physical harm arising to the person of another, or (3) to render assistance to another after that other has suffered serious physical harm".

It has been held that in New Zealand that the equivalent of a "999" call gives the police authority to enter private property based on necessity (*R v Fraser* [2005] 2 N.Z.L.R. 109, following the approach of the Supreme Court of Canada in *R. v Godoy* [1999] 1 S.C.R. 311).

CHAPTER 7

Lawful Justifications for Entry, Search and Seizure

ENTRY AND SEARCH WITHOUT WARRANT

Entry and search at common law

Entry to deal with a breach of the peace

7–008   In *Friswell v Chief Constable of Essex Police* [2004] EWHC QB 3009, Cox J. held that only exceptional circumstances could justify entry onto premises to prevent a breach of the peace: the officer had to be satisfied there was a real and imminent threat of a breach of the peace of sufficient gravity to justify entry.

Search of premises occupied by a person under arrest

7–011   The premises of a person under arrest may only be searched under the common law when the person was arrested "in the curtilage" of the property which is his home (it is not sufficient that he keeps goods there and occasionally stays overnight) and without undue delay (see *Hewitson v Chief Constable of Dorset Police* [2003] EWHC Admin 3296, at [25]–[36].

Entry and search under PACE: preliminary matters

Reasonable force

7–017   In *Friswell v Chief Constable of Essex Police* [2004] EWHC QB 3009, Cox J. held that an important factor in assessing whether force was necessary to enter premises under powers given by s.17 of PACE was whether the officer explained the reason why entry was required.

In *DPP v Meaden* [2004] 1 W.L.R. 945, the Divisional Court held that the   7–018
police were entitled on the facts of the case to use reasonable force to prevent a
person moving about a property being searched and to detain him in a bath-
room and then a bedroom. This was founded on the broad proposition that a
warrant "to be meaningful, had . . . to enable the search to be effective" rather
than on the suggestion made by Sedley L.J. in *Hepburn v Chief Constable of
Thames Valley* that a deprivation of liberty could only be justified as an arrest
for obstructing a police officer the execution of his duty. This suggestion was
held to be based on the false premise that obstructing a police officer was an
arrestable offence (see paras 12–13 and 29). Rose L.J. held that:

> "Although I accept it is for the police to show, and the burden upon them is
> a heavy one, that the use of force was necessary and reasonable, it seems to
> me to be entirely reasonable that officers should seek, by no more force than
> is necessary, to restrict the movement of those in occupation of premises,
> while those premises are being searched." (para.32)

Because the premises in question were over two floors and were occupied by a
number of people, the police were entitled to restrict the movement of those
people while the search was carried out. The Divisional Court distinguished
Hepburn on the basis that that the warrant permitted the search not just of the
premises, but also of persons within it (in relation to which there is a specific
power to detain under s.23 of PACE). But it seems from the judgments that the
court would in any event have found that the search of the premises alone could
justify restricting the movement of persons within it.

Entry and search under PACE: the powers

2. To arrest for an arrestable offence

When para.24 of Sch.7 to the Serious Organised Crime and Police Act 2005 is   7–023
brought into force by order of the Secretary of State, the concept of an
"arrestable offence" will be removed from PACE (see Supplement, para.5–048,
above). By para.43(4) of Sch.7 to the 2005 Act, the power under s.17(1)(b) will
be exercisable in relation to an indictable offence.

7. To search premises where a person was when arrested

By para.43(6) of Sch.7 to the Serious Organised Crime and Police Act 2005,   7–036
which will come into force on a date appointed by the Secretary of State, the
power under s.17(1)(b) will be exercisable only in relation to indictable offences.

SEIZURE WITHOUT WARRANT

Police powers of seizure under statute

Other PACE powers of seizure

7–049 **Evidence found on premises of person under arrest** When para.24 of Sch.7 to the Serious Organised Crime and Police Act 2005 is brought into force by order of the Secretary of State, the concept of an "arrestable offence" will be removed from PACE (see para.5–048 above). By para.43(5) of Sch.7 to the 2005 Act, the power under s.18 will be exercisable in relation to indictable offences.

Seizure of large quantities of goods and sifting

Sifting

7–058 In *International Paper Converters Limited v Chief Constable of City of London Police* [2004] EWHC QB 957, however, Poole J. noted that "the fact that another person some time later concludes that [certain of the seized goods] do not assist the investigation does not mean they were outside the warrant or were not reasonably thought to be evidence of an offence".

RETENTION, ACCESS AND COPYING

Retention of seized items

7–065 The entitlement of the police to retain seized goods was fully considered by the Court of Appeal in *Gough v Chief Constable of West Midlands Police* [2004] EWCA Civ 206. The police kept in their possession cannibalised parts of cars, seized from the claimant. The police believed them to be stolen, while the claimant claimed that he had obtained them lawfully as wrecked vehicles. The police initially intended to commence proceedings in the magistrates' court, under the Police (Property) Act 1897, for an order as to who should retain the property. However, when the claimant commenced civil proceedings in the county court, they abandoned any such intention. It was held that the retention of the goods was unlawful. Park J. stated the general principles in the following terms:

"first, that if the police are holding property which they have seized from some other person who was previously in possession of it, they can only resist a civil claim by the former possessor for its return if they can identify a statutory power to retain it [though it may be that the police could also rely on a common law power: see *Civil Actions Against the Police* (3rd ed.), paras 7–063 and 7–064]; second, that if the original seizure was authorised by a statutory power, it does not necessarily follow that indefinite detention of the property continues to be authorised by the statutory power; third, that a civil claim by the former possessor, brought under the Torts (Interference with Goods) Act 1977, is determined by common law principles deriving from the law of detinue and conversion; fourth, that, if the police do not have a continuing statutory power or right to retain the property, the former possessor's right of possession is superior to theirs; and fifth, that it is no defence for the police to argue that the former possessor, the claimant in the civil action, is not the true owner of the property. On the fifth point it may be different if the police can establish who the true owner is (I say nothing about a case where that is so) . . ." ([15])

Park J. accepted that while the police genuinely intended to use the procedure under the Police (Property) Act 1897, there was an implied statutory power to retain the goods pending the decision of the magistrates (see [27] and see also [32]). However, such a power did not exist in relation to a civil claim: the mere fact that the police contested the claimant's right to the goods did not entitle them to retain those goods: see [33]. Accordingly, when the police abandoned the 1897 Act procedure, they could not rely on any implied right to keep the goods. Park J. thought that they were right to abandon the 1897 Act procedure, but there was some disagreement amongst the court as to the proper use of that Act: see Supplement, paras 15–056 and 15–058, below.

As for the express statutory powers to retain goods under s.22 of PACE, the police could not rely on s.22(2)(b) and say that they were retaining the goods in order to establish their lawful owner, as there was no realistic prospect of the lawful owners being established and there was no evidence of any continuing attempts to trace them: see [29]. Moreover, it could only be "necessary" to retain goods under s.22(1) in "circumstances which are associated with the law enforcement functions of the police". 7–065A

In *Settelen v Commissioner of Police for the Metropolis* [2004] EWHC Ch 2171, at [56], Peter Smith J. held that whether it was necessary to retain goods "involves an investigation on a case-by-case, fact-by-fact basis": 7–065B

"Where the property is seized is that of the person charged with the offences, or being investigated in relation to those goods, very little evidence will be required to justify a retention. On the other hand, as both the common law cases and the statute clearly intended in my judgment where the goods and property of third parties is involved a balancing exercise can and should take place. For example, if the police seize a very valuable asset belonging to an innocent person, which was needed for that person to carry on its business, I cannot see that a retention of that piece of property is going to be justified (assuming it cannot be copied) if safe guards can be put in place to preserve the item whilst allowing it to remain in the possession of the innocent third party."

On the basis that the claimant had offered undertakings to preserve the relevant items—videotapes, taken by him, of Diana, Princess of Wales, which were implicated in an alleged theft by her former butler—and the police had not indicated that this arrangement would cause them any concern from the point of view of preservation, the retention of those tapes was not "necessary". The judgment also makes clear that the police are no more entitled to retain copies of seized items than originals.

ENTRY, SEARCH AND SEIZURE UNDER WARRANT

Access to excluded and special procedure material

7–085
to 7–097

Magistrates will have new powers to grant warrants to search any premises occupied or controlled by a person specified in the application by virtue of s.113(10)–(15) of the Serious Organised Crime and Police Act 2005. Moreover, by para.43(13) of Sch.7 to that Act, a production order may be issued under para.2 of Sch.1 to PACE in relation to an indictable offence, rather than the higher threshold of a "serious arrestable offence". These provisions will come into force on a date to be appointed. See further Supplement, paras 7–089 to 7–122, below.

Access to other material

7–098
to 7–102

The Serious Organised Crime and Police Act 2005 ("SOCPA") will significantly extend the powers of magistrates to grant search orders when s.113 and para.43(3) of Sch.7 are brought into force by the Secretary of State. There are three main changes:

- a magistrate will be able to issue a warrant if there are reasonable grounds to believe that an indictable offence (rather than a serious arrestable offence) has been committed: see para.43(3) of Sch.7 to SOCPA. This is a significantly lower threshold,

- a magistrate will have power to issue "all premises" warrants to search any premises occupied or controlled by a person specified on the warrant: see s.113(4) of SOCPA inserting a new s.8(1B)(a) into PACE. This will include but will not be limited to particular premises specified on the warrant. There are additional requirements put in place to govern the use of this power. The application must specify:

- as many sets of premises which it is desired to enter and search as is reasonably practicable to specify,
- the person who is in occupation or control of those premises and any others which it is desired to enter and search,
- why it is necessary to search more premises than those that have been specified, and
- why it is not reasonably practicable to specify all the premises which it is desired to enter and search.

The magistrate must be satisfied that, because of the particulars of the offence specified in the application, there are reasonable grounds for believing that it is necessary to search unspecified premises occupied or controlled by that person in order to find the material which is likely to be of substantial value to the investigation *and* that it is not reasonably practicable to specify in the application all the premises which he occupies or controls and which might need to be searched. Moreover, those premises which are unspecified can only be entered or searched with the written authorisation of a police officer of at least the rank of inspector. (See ss.113(4), (8) and (9) of SOCPA, inserting ss.8(1B) and (2A) and 16(3A) of PACE.) Similar new powers to grant "all premises" warrants will be conferred in relation to special procedure material and excluded material by s.113(10)–(15) of SOCPA. For the current powers in relation to such material see para.7–085 *Civil Actions Against the Police* (3rd ed.).

- magistrates will be able to issue "multiple entry" warrants, namely warrants which authorise the search of premises on more than one occasion. There is no limit on the number of searches which can be authorised, though the warrant must be returned after three months by virtue of new s.16(10A) of PACE. The application must state the ground on which the police officer applies for such a warrant, and whether he seeks a warrant authorising unlimited entries, or (if not) the maximum number of entries he desires. The justice of the peace must be satisfied that it is necessary to authorise multiple entries in order to achieve the purpose for which he issues the warrant, which must specify whether an unlimited number of entries are authorised and (if not) the number of entries authorised. Again, any multiple entry under the same warrant must be authorised in writing by a police officer of at least the rank of inspector. (See s.114 of SOCPA, inserting ss.8(1C) and (1D), 15(5A) and 16(3B), and amending s.15(2)(a)(iii) of PACE.)

There are very real doubts as to whether such extensive search and entry powers are compatible with the Convention: see the *Scrutiny Fourth Progress Report* by the Joint Committee on Human Rights (HL Paper 60, HC 388), February 23, 2005, especially paras 1.91–1.96. The Committee was not satisfied that the new provisions were compatible with Art.8, noting that:

"the clauses give justices of the peace authority to issue a general warrant of a kind that has been anathema to the common law for centuries on account of the very wide discretion it confers on public officials, and the lack of effective prior judicial control over the decision to enter (if need be, by force) private premises including dwellings. . .

". . . safeguards external to the police are weak, because the justice of the peace is very unlikely to be able to assess properly the proportionality of a request to be allowed to enter and search unspecified premises on an unlimited number of future occasions over the following three months; and decisions of an inspector in relation to particular premises are unlikely to be subject to judicial or public scrutiny . . ."

Procedure for applying for warrants

7–109   The problems which arise under the present practice are illustrated by the case of *International Paper Converters Limited v Chief Constable of City of London Police* [2004] EWHC QB 957, the claimant alleged that the police had withheld important information from the magistrates in the without notice application. Poole J. noted (at [30]) that "the evidence of the justices' clerk is far from conclusive. In the absence of a shorthand record, there can be no certainty in the matter". He had to rely on the evidence given by the police officer concerned in the claim before him and concluded "on the balance of probabilities that there is no substantial reason to suppose that the wider information was not given to the justices".

7–109A   It now appears that the preference expressed by the Court of Appeal in *R v Marylebone Magistrates, Ex p. Amdrell Ltd.* (1998) 162 J.P. 719 and the Divisional Court in *R. (Cronin) v Sheffield Justices* [2003] 1 W.L.R. 752 (that magistrates should make a note of any additional evidence not contained in the Information and should give reasons for the issue of a warrant) is in fact a requirement under Art.8 of the Convention, at least where the full reasons for the grant of the warrant are not obvious on the face of the Information: see *Cronin v UK* (Decision of January 6, 2004). It is suggested that, when the new more extensive search warrant powers conferred by SOCPA (see paras 7–098 to 7–102, above) come into force, a note of the evidence and reasons for the grant of the warrant will be essential.

7–109B   In *R. (Energy Financing Team Ltd) v Director of Serious Fraud Office* [2005] EWHC Admin 1626, in a case involving a warrant following a request for further assistance, the Divisional Court drew a number of general conclusions from the authorities which, it is submitted, apply in all warrant cases:

- "the grant and execution of a warrant to search and seize is a serious infringement of the liberty of the subject, which needs to be clearly justified and before seeking or granting a warrant is always necessary to consider whether some lesser measure . . . will suffice" (at [24(1)]).

- "If an application is to be made for a warrant it is the duty of the applicant to give full assistance to the District Judge and that includes drawing to his or her attention anything that militates against the issue of a warrant" (at [24(3)]).

- "the warrant needs to be drafted with sufficient precision to enable both those who execute it and those whose property is affected by it to know whether any individual document or class or documents falls within it" (at [24(5)]).

- "If the applicant supplements the material already provided, possibly in response to questions from the District Judge, that should be noted, and the same applies to the decision of the District Judge, which should be briefly reasoned. It seems that sometimes proceedings before the District Judge are tape-recorded, and if that can be arranged that is clearly the best form of record, but if that is impracticable the party applying for a warrant must prepare a note which can be submitted to the judge for approval if any issue arises as to they way in which the warrant was obtained" (at [24(7)]).

- "The remedy which is available to a person or persons affected by a warrant is to seek judicial review. It is an adequate remedy because the statutory provisions have to be read in the light of those Articles of the European Convention which are now part of English law" (at [24(9)].

- "the person affected has a right to be satisfied as to the legality of the procedure which led to the execution of the warrant, and if he or his representatives do ask to see what was laid before the District Judge and to be told what happened at the hearing, there should, so far as possible, be an accommodating response to that request. It is not sufficient to say that the applicant was adequately protected because discretion has been exercised first by the Director and then by the District Judge" (at 24(10)).

A warrant should be capable of being understood by those carrying out the search and by those whose premises are being searched, without reference to any other document (*R. (Energy Financing Team Ltd) v Director of Serious Fraud Office* [2005] EWHC Admin 1626 at [37], *per* Crane J.   7–110

Procedure for executing warrants

The Divisional Court held in *R (Kent Pharmaceuticals Ltd) v Director of Serious Fraud Office* [2003] EWHC Admin 3002 at [18], that, where a warrant limits the scope of documents to be seized to those produced within a particular time period, an officer is entitled to resolve any doubts about whether a   7–116 highly relevant document falls within that time period in favour of seizing the document and will, if he does so, have reasonable grounds for his belief. The case was appealed on a different point: [2005] 1 All E.R. 449.

7–118   For an example of a case where police lawfully on premises under a warrant were entitled to seize items under s.19(2) of PACE, see *International Paper Converters Limited v Chief Constable of City of London Police* [2004] EWHC QB 957. (In fact, the judge appears to have proceeded on the erroneous basis that s.19(2) entitled a police officer to seize items he reasonably believed to be "evidence" of an offence. It actually permits seizure of items which the officer has reasonable grounds for believing were obtained in consequence of the commission of an offence: see *Civil Actions Against the Police* (3rd ed.), para.7–044.)

CHALLENGING SEARCH WARRANTS

Introduction

7–125A   If a challenge is not made to a justices' warrant then a constable who acts in obedience to its terms is protected against action by s.6 of the Constables Protection Act 1750 (see *Civil Actions Against the Police* (3rd ed.), paras 3–035 and 5–111ff). There are, however, two broad limitations on this rule:

- the officer must act in a way reasonably calculated to achieve his purpose of searching pursuant to the warrant, so that excessive unauthorised or unreasonable behaviour loses him the protection of s.6: see for instance *Price v Messenger* (1800) 2 Bos. & P. 158;

- an officer may be liable if there is a formal defect on the face of the warrant sufficiently grave to invalidate it"

(see *Bell v Chief Constable of Greater Manchester* QBD, April 27, 2005, Cooke J.).

POLICE POWERS IN RELATION TO VEHICLES

Road checks

7–163   Para.43(2) of Sch.3 to the Serious Organised Crime and Police Act 2005, which will come into force on a date appointed by the Secretary of State under s.178 of the Act, will replace the term "serious arrestable offence" in s.4 of PACE with "indictable offence", thereby enlarging the number of offences in relation to which a road block may be set up.

ENTRY, SEARCH AND SEIZURE AND THE CONVENTION

Article 8

Introduction

As well as covering a private individual's residence, the word "home" in Art.8   **7–174A**
also covers a company's registered office, branches and other business premises
(see, for example, *Buck v Germany,* Judgment of April 28, 2005, para.31; *van
Rossem v Belgium* Judgment of December 9, 2004, para.36).

In determining whether a search is "necessary in a democratic society" under   **7–174B**
Art.8 the Court must first ensure that the relevant legislation and practice afford
individuals adequate and effective safeguards against abuse. The Court must
then consider, whether, in all the circumstances, the interference in question was
proportionate to the aim pursued. The Court will take into account matters
such as:

- the severity of the offence in connection with which the search and seizure was effected,

- the manner and circumstances in which the order had been issued, in particular further evidence available at that time,

- the content and scope of the order, having particular regard to the nature of the premises searched and the safeguards taken in order to confine the impact of the measure to reasonable bounds, and the extent of possible repercussions on the reputation of the person affected by the search

(see generally, *Buck v Germany,* Judgment of April 28, 2005, para.45).

Procedural protections

In *Cronin v UK* (Decision of January 6, 2004) the European Court of Human   **7–175**
Rights held that the procedure for issuing a warrant on the facts of that case
was compatible with Art.8 of the Convention. However, it is important to note
that this decision was based on the fact that:

"in this case the Information laid before the justices can be regarded as containing all the relevant material on which they based their decision and. . . the
applicant was in a position to assess whether the procedure for the grant of
the warrant had been properly adhered to, given that he had access to the
Information. As the Lord Chief Justice observed, giving judgment in the
Divisional Court [in *R. (Cronin) v Sheffield Justices* [2003] 1 W.L.R. 752], it
may well be that in an appropriate case, additional reasons, or a fuller note

of the questions asked of the constable by the justices would be necessary to satisfy the procedural requirements . . .".

It is suggested that, in light of this, there can be little doubt that where magistrates obtain additional information from the constable applying for a warrant, or issue the warrant for reasons not obvious on the face of the Information, they should record this in writing. The note of evidence and the reasons given should be made available to the claimant on request—unless the criminal investigation is continuing and disclosure might prejudice the investigation (see the discussion in R. *(Energy Financing Team Ltd) v Director of Serious Fraud Office* [2005] EWHC Admin 1626 at [24].

CHAPTER 8

Malicious Prosecution and Related Actions

MALICIOUS PROSECUTION: INTRODUCTION

The role of the jury

8–013   For jury questions in negligence cases, see Supplement, new para.3–138A, above.

THE PROSECUTION

The defendant's role

8–026   The Canadian courts have taken a broad approach to the question of whether a person is a prosecutor. The Manitoba Court of Queen's Bench suggested in *AAD v Tanner* [2004] C.R.D.J. 3467, para.106, that "an informant may be regarded as a prosecutor if his information virtually compels the police to prosecute, even more where he deliberately deceives the police by supplying false information without which they would not have proceeded". In the case of *Tschekalin v Brunette* [2004] O.J. 2855, the Ontario Superior Court of Justice held that a person may be a prosecutor if he gives the police a false statement, even if it does not implicate any particular person, if he fails to correct or withdraw that statement when he knows that someone has been arrested as a result of it. In that case, the defendant claimed he had been shot by a bearded man in a dark van. The police subsequently arrested a man on suspicion of this offence, but it later transpired that the defendant had concocted the whole story and had in fact shot himself. It was held that he was liable for malicious prosecution: see para.85.

FAVOURABLE TERMINATION OF THE PROSECUTION

Introduction

8–032   In Canada, the withdrawal of charges on the agreement of defendant to pay a sum of money to a charity does not amount to a favourable termination of a prosecution: see *Hunt v Ontario* [2004] O.J. 5284, Ontario Superior Court of Justice, para.16. This does not represent the law in England and Wales: see *Craig v Hassell* (1843) 4 Q.B. 481 and *Hourihane v Commissioner of Police for the Metropolis, Independent*, January 18, 1995.

LACK OF REASONABLE AND PROBABLE CAUSE

Introduction

In *Paul v Chief Constable of Humberside Police* [2004] EWCA Civ 308, at [44], 8–042 the Court of Appeal held that "a claimant cannot ordinarily be expected to produce direct evidence" of the absence of reasonable and probable cause (or malice) and approved the following statement from the judgment of the Privy Council in *Gibbs v Rea* [1998] A.C. 786:

> "The motives of parties can only be ascertained by inference drawn from facts. The want of probable cause is, in some degree, a negative, and the plaintiff can only be called upon to give some. . . slight evidence of such want . . .".

The judgment emphasises that judges should not be too ready to withhold questions relating to the absence of reasonable and probable cause from the jury: (see paras 43, 52, and 58).

The Northern Ireland High Court has also made clear that weak evidence may support an inference of reasonable and probable cause (see *Maccionaith v Chief Constable of the RUC* [2003] N.I.Q.B. 53, para.49). However, Kerr J. warned against retrospective reasoning: even though the magistrate had characterised the prosecution evidence when the case came to court as "nebulous and flimsy", it does not necessarily follow that this had been exposed at the time of the decision to prosecute.

The questions for the jury

The Court of Appeal offered a formulation of what the prosecutor needs to 8–048 believe in *Coudrat v Commissioners of Customs & Excise* [2005] EWCA Civ 616, at [41]: "an officer is entitled to lay a charge if he is satisfied that there is a case fit to be tried. He does not have to believe in the probability of conviction".

The questions for the judge

The matters which the prosecutor should take into account before proceeding 8–052 were considered in *Coudrat v Commissioners of Customs & Excise* [2005] EWCA Civ 616, at [42] and [46]. The Court of Appeal held that:

"When considering whether to charge a suspect, consideration must be given to the elements of the offence with which it is intended to charge him. There must be prima facie admissible evidence of each element of the offence. Although anything plainly inadmissible should be left out of account, we do not think that, at the stage of charging, it is necessary or appropriate to consider the possibility that evidence might be excluded at the trial after full legal argument or in the exercise of the judge's discretion. Nor is it necessary to test the full strength of the defence. An officer cannot be expected to investigate the truth of every assertion made by the suspect in interview. . . .

. . . To justify the charge there had to be prima facie evidence . . ., that is evidence which, unless successfully refuted or explained, could lead a reasonable jury to be satisfied of the appellant's [guilt] . . .".

8–056   Just as counsel's advice that there is sufficient evidence to prosecute is not conclusive of the existence of reasonable and probable cause, is counsel's advice that there was insufficient evidence to secure a conviction is not necessarily indicative of a lack of reasonable and probable cause or the presence of malice (see *Coudrat*, at [56]).

MALICE

Definition

8–066   It has been said that:

"a suit for malicious prosecution must be based on more than recklessness or gross negligence. Rather, it requires evidence that reveals a wilful and intentional effort on the Crown's part to abuse or distort its proper role within the criminal justice system. . . . The key to a malicious prosecution is malice, but the concept of malice in this context includes prosecutorial conduct that is fuelled by an "improper purpose" or, . . . a purpose "inconsistent with the status of 'minister of justice'". (*Proulx v Quebec (Attorney-General)* [2001] 3 S.C.R. 9, para.35).

n.19: For a discussion of malice in the context of malicious prosecution see the decisions of the Supreme Court of Canada in *Nelles v. Ontario* [1989] 2 S.C.R. 170, 193 and *Proulx v Quebec (Attorney-General)* [2001] 3 S.C.R. 9.

Proof of malice

8–071   In the Canadian case of *DK v Miazga* ([2003] S.J. 830), the judge of the Saskatchewan Court of Queen's Bench inferred malice from a number of facts, including: a failure properly to appraise the evidence (para.141); an overlong period of custody (para.176); the lack of reasonable and probable cause (para. 381); the lack of subsequent regret and remorse (para.405); and an over-aggressive prosecution (para.416; though the judge considered it would be rare that this could properly sustain a finding of malice).

CHAPTER 9

Police Surveillance and Information Gathering

COMMON LAW REMEDIES

Breach of confidence

Misuse of private information

In *Campbell v MGN* ([2004] 2 A.C. 457) the House of Lords recognised that the law of breach of confidence has moved forward and that, while there is no over-arching cause of action for invasion of privacy, the law of breach of confidence now in reality protects "private information". The House was split on the outcome of the case, a majority holding that publication of details of drug addiction treatment obtained by Naomi Campbell, the famous fashion model, and a photograph of her leaving a session, was unlawful. However, in relation to the law lords' exposition of the law, Lord Hoffmann expressed the view that "the principles are expressed in varying language but speaking for myself I can see no significant differences" (para.36). Lord Nicholls summarised the position in this way:

9–018A

> "In this country, unlike the United States of America, there is no over-arching, all-embracing cause of action for 'invasion of privacy' . . . But protection of various aspects of privacy is a fast developing area of the law, here and in some other common law jurisdictions . . .
>
> The present case concerns one aspect of invasion of privacy: wrongful disclosure of private information. The case involves the familiar competition between freedom of expression and respect for an individual's privacy . . .
>
> The common law or, more precisely, courts of equity have long afforded protection to the wrongful use of private information by means of the cause of action which became known as breach of confidence. A breach of confidence was restrained as a form of unconscionable conduct, akin to a breach of trust. Today this nomenclature is misleading. The breach of confidence label harks back to the time when the cause of action was based on improper use of information disclosed by one person to another in confidence. To attract protection the information had to be of a confidential nature. But the gist of the cause of action was that information of this character had been disclosed by one person to another in circumstances 'importing an obligation of confidence' . . .
>
> This cause of action has now firmly shaken off the limiting constraint of the need for an initial confidential relationship. In doing so it has changed its nature. In this country this development was recognised clearly in the judgment of Lord Goff of Chieveley in *Attorney General v Guardian Newspapers Ltd (No 2)* [1990] 1 AC 109, 281. Now the law imposes a 'duty of confidence' whenever a person receives information he knows or ought to know is fairly and reasonably to be regarded as confidential. Even this formulation is awkward. The continuing use of the phrase 'duty of confidence' and the

description of the information as 'confidential' is not altogether comfortable. Information about an individual's private life would not, in ordinary usage, be called 'confidential'. The more natural description today is that such information is private. The essence of the tort is better encapsulated now as misuse of private information ...". (paras 11–15).

9–018B   What, then, is "private"? It seems that the test is a relatively broad one. Lord Nicholls's opinion (paras 21–22) was that:

"in deciding what was the ambit of an individual's 'private life' in particular circumstances courts need to be on guard against using as a touchstone a test which brings into account considerations which should more properly be considered at the later stage of proportionality. Essentially the touchstone of private life is whether in respect of the disclosed facts the person in question had a reasonable expectation of privacy.

Different forms of words, usually to much the same effect, have been suggested from time to time. The *American Law Institute, Restatement of the Law, Torts*, (2nd ed., 1977), section 652D, uses the formulation of disclosure of matter which 'would be highly offensive to a reasonable person'. In *Australian Broadcasting Corpn v Lenah Game Meats Pty Ltd* (2001) 208 C.L.R. 199, 226, para.42, Gleeson C.J. used words, widely quoted, having a similar meaning. This particular formulation should be used with care, for two reasons. First, the 'highly offensive' phrase is suggestive of a stricter test of private information than a reasonable expectation of privacy. Second, the 'highly offensive' formulation can all too easily bring into account, when deciding whether the disclosed information was private, considerations which go more properly to issues of proportionality; for instance, the degree of intrusion into private life, and the extent to which publication was a matter of proper public concern. This could be a recipe for confusion."

9–018C   The Court of Appeal put it more broadly in *Douglas and Zeta-Jones v Hello!* [2005] EWCA Civ 595. Lord Phillips M.R., giving the judgment of the court, accepted the validity of Lord Nicholls's comments about the description of the tort cited above, and held that:

"for the adjective 'confidential' one can substitute the word 'private'. What is the nature of 'private' information? It seems to us that it must include information that is personal to the person who possesses it and that he does not intend shall be imparted to the general public. The nature of the information, or the form in which it is kept, may suffice to make it plain that the information satisfies these criteria."

The Court held that the United Kingdom's Art.8 obligations to protect individuals from unjustified intrusion of private life had to be performed by adopting "the cause of action formerly described as breach of confidence" as a vehicle (at [53]). As a result:

> "knowledge, actual or imputed, that information is private will normally impose on anyone publishing that information the duty to justify what, in the absence of justification, will be a wrongful invasion of privacy" (at [82]).

It is no longer necessary for the information to have been imparted in circumstances "importing a duty of confidence".

Once it is decided that the information in question is "private", then a bal-   9–018D
ancing act in the nature of that required by Art.8 of the European Convention on Human Rights is to be carried out to determine whether the disclosure or use of that information was proportionate and legitimate (see *Campbell*, especially paras 20–21 and 137). In the *Campbell* case this involved the difficult task of balancing the media's right to freedom of expression against the claimant's right to privacy. Freedom of expression will not always be the primary consideration for disclosure (see, for example, the comments of Lady Hale in *Campbell*, para.142) and in police cases broader considerations of the public interest may often arise, most notably perhaps the public interest in an open criminal justice system and in the detection and prevention of crime.

Disclosure of information by public bodies

The Court of Appeal reconfirmed the need for a particular public interest to   9–022
justify disclosure of information by the police in *Wood v Chief Constable of the West Midlands Police* [2005] E.M.L.R. 20. Referring to *R. v Chief Constable of North Wales Police, Ex p Thorpe*, May L.J. held that:

> "the police have a job to do. They should not generally disclose damaging information, other than for the purpose [of] and to the extent necessary for the performance of their public duties. They have a duty to detect and prevent crime and protect potential victims of crime. The principle does not prevent factual statements about police operations, even if such a statement includes a report that an individual has been arrested or charged [though see *Civil Actions Against the Police* (3rd ed.), para.9–092]. Any disclosure must be properly considered at an appropriate level of seniority. Disclosure of damaging information about individuals requires specific public interest justification. Ill-considered and indiscriminate disclosure is scarcely likely to measure up to this standard." (at [63])

In that case, defamatory letters sent to insurance brokers warning them that an individual had been charged with a criminal offence and anticipating that he would be convicted could not be justified by the defence of qualified privilege:

they did not sufficiently contribute to the prevention of crime or the protection of victims to justify disclosure.

9–22A   Where a statutory scheme provides for disclosure in particular circumstances, it may be that the scheme itself demonstrates the "pressing need" and that no further particular public interest need be sought. In R. (X) v Chief Constable of the West Midlands Police [2005] 1 W.L.R. 65, the Court of Appeal approved R. v Chief Constable of North Wales Police, Ex p. Thorpe and R. v Local Authority in the Midlands, Ex p LM but did not consider it appropriate to apply such a general approach to the issue of an Enhanced Criminal Record Certificate. A statutory scheme under the Police Act 1997 provides for the issue of these Certificates by the Secretary of State in relation to persons applying for employment which involves, among other things, regularly caring for persons under 18. The Court held that a chief constable was obliged by s.115 of the 1997 Act to disclose to the Secretary of State any information which he considered might be relevant and that this was compatible with Art.8 because the public interest in relevant information being made available to the employer outweighed the potential damage to the individual concerned. Accordingly, contrary to the usual position, there was here a presumption in *favour* of disclosure if the information was relevant and no specific justification was required (see para.36). The question of whether or not information was relevant was for the chief constable, not the court, and there was no requirement to allow the individual to make representations before disclosure (see paras 36–41 and 46–47). However, the Court accepted that:

> "it is possible that there could be cases where the information should not be included in the certificate because it is disproportionate to do so; the information might be as to some trifling matter; it may be that the evidence made it so unlikely that the information was correct, that it again would be disproportionate to disclose it."

The House of Lords refused permission to appeal [2005] 1 W.L.R. 2004.

The invasion of Privacy

Introduction

9–030A   The English law has now recognised a tort of "misuse of private information", see Supplement, para.9–18A, above.

9–030B   In *Douglas v Hello!* [2005] EWCA Civ 595, the Court of Appeal dealt with what it described as the "special considerations" attaching to photographs in the field of privacy. It made three important points. First, photographs are not merely a method of conveying information that is an alternative to verbal description:

"They enable the person viewing the photograph to act as a spectator, in some circumstances voyeur would be the more appropriate noun, of whatever it is that the photograph depicts". (at [84])

Second, insofar as a photograph does more than convey information and intrudes on privacy by enabling the viewer to focus on intimate personal detail, there will be a fresh intrusion of privacy when each additional viewer sees the photograph and even when one who has seen a previous publication of the photograph, is confronted by a fresh publication of it. An injunction can be granted to restrain further publication in appropriate cases (at [105]). Third, a personal photograph can portray, not necessarily accurately, the personality and the mood of the subject of the photograph. It is quite wrong to suppose that a person who authorises publication of selected personal photographs taken on a private occasion, will not reasonably feel distress at the publication of unauthorised photographs taken on the same occasion (at [106]).

EUROPEAN CONVENTION ON HUMAN RIGHTS

The Human Rights Act 1998

The House of Lords has now confirmed in *Campbell v MGN* [2004] 2 A.C. 457, that the principles underlying Art.8 (the right to privacy) and the sometimes-competing rights conferred by Art.10 (the right to freedom of expression) are fully reflected in the common law principles of breach of confidence or "misuse of private information" (see Supplement, paras 9–018Aff, above). They therefore apply as much to private individuals as to public authorities. However, at present, this applies only misuse of private information: Article 8 does not require the courts to develop a general tort of invasion of privacy.   **9–034**

Another example of a case where the publication of photographs—even of famous figures, in this case Princess Caroline of Monaco—was held to breach Art.8 is *von Hannover v Germany* [2004] E.M.L.R. 21. This case, concerned paparazzi photographs taken and published to satiate public interest in Princess Caroline but the European Court of Human Rights made a number of comments which of some broader relevance. The Court said that "increased vigilance in protecting private life is necessary to contend with new communication technologies which make it possible to store and reproduce personal data" (at [70]). The Court also acknowledged that "the context in which these photos were taken—without the applicant's knowledge or consent" was a factor to be put into the balance when considering whether publication was justified (at [68]).   **9–036**

THE REGULATION OF INVESTIGATORY POWERS ACT 2000

Introduction

9–042 RIPA regulates interests which the Telecommunications and Data Protection Director 97/66 requires to be protected and is compatible with it (*R. v E.* (2004) 2 Cr. App. R. 29).

Overview of provisions

9–044 A recording of someone speaking into a mobile phone by surveillance device in a person's car is not an "interception" for the purposes of RIPA (*R. v E.* (2004) 2 Cr. App. R. 29).

DATA PROTECTION

Introduction

General

9–059 The question as to whether information is data is to be answered at the time of the data request (*Johnson v Medical Defence Union* [2004] EWHC Ch 347). Data does not form part of a relevant filing system simply because it could be turned into a computer database (*Smith v Lloyds TSB Bank* [2005] EWHC Ch 246).

Data protection principles

9–065 In order to be "personal data" for the purposes of the DPA the information must relate to a living individual who can be identified from the data: it must be "biographical in a significant sense" and must have the individual as its focus (see generally, *Durant v Financial Services Authority* [2004] F.S.R. 28).

SURVEILLANCE, INFORMATION AND THE POLICE

The police and confidential information

Introduction

As to the general principles concerning disclosure of information by the police, see also *Wood v Chief Constable of the West Midlands Police* [2005] E.M.L.R. 20 (see Supplement, para.9–022, above).

9–082

Disclosure of police photographs

In relation to the disclosure of photographs, see generally *Douglas v Hello!* [2005] EWCA Civ 595 (Supplement, para.9–030B, above).

9–086

Breach of confidence claims

The first claim for breach of confidence by an informant to reach the courts was *X & Y v Chief Constable of Greater Manchester Police* [2004] EWHC QB 764. The claimants, X and Y, were a police informant whose identity had been disclosed to defendants in criminal proceedings in breach of undertakings of confidentiality, and his partner. After this disclosure the claimant and his partner were treated as though they were on the witness protection scheme and were relocated with new identities. The police admitted liability and the claimants were awarded damages for disruption to their lives and for psychiatric injury. X was awarded £25,000 and Y was awarded £32,500.

9–090

CHAPTER 10

Negligence

DUTY OF CARE

Introduction

In *D v East Berkshire Health Authority* [2005] 2 W.L.R. 993, the House of Lords   **10–004**
considered the argument the notion of a "duty of care" is superfluous and the
bounds of negligence claims can be properly contained by the application of an
appropriate standard of care. Lord Nicholls considered that "this radical suggestion is not without attraction", but took the view that removal of the
requirement for a duty of care would lead to uncertainty (paras 92–94).

The general principles behind the notion of a "duty of care" are helpfully set   **10–005**
out by Lord Nicholls in *Attorney-General v Hartwell* [2004] 1 W.L.R. 1273, PC:

"Negligence as a basis of liability is founded on the impersonal ('objective')
standard of how a reasonable person should have acted in the circumstances.
Shortfall from this standard of conduct does not always give rise to legal liability. In order to elucidate the circumstances in which shortfall will give rise
to liability the courts have fashioned several concepts, such as 'duty of care'.
This familiar phrase is legal shorthand. Expressed more fully, a duty of care
is a duty owed in law by one person or class of persons to another particular
person or class of persons. The duty comprises an obligation to take reasonable care to ensure that the person or persons to whom the duty is owed do
not suffer a particular type or types of damage. Thus drivers of cars owe,
among other duties, a duty to other road users to take reasonable care to
avoid inflicting personal injury on the latter.

Speaking generally, one of the necessary prerequisites for the existence of
a duty of care is foresight that carelessness on the part of the defendant may
cause damage of a particular kind to the plaintiff. Was it reasonably foresee-
able that, failing the exercise of reasonable care, harm of the relevant description might be suffered by the plaintiff or members of a class including the
plaintiff? 'Might be suffered' embraces a wide range of degrees of possibility,
from the highly probable to the possible but highly improbable. Bearing in
mind that the underlying concept is fairness and reasonableness, the degree
of likelihood needed to satisfy this prerequisite depends upon the circumstances of the case. Reasonable foreseeability does not denote a fixed point
on the scale of probability: see Lord Hoffmann in *Jolley v Sutton London
Borough Council* [2000] 1 WLR 1082, 1091. There must be reasonable foreseeability of a risk which a reasonable person would not ignore. The risk
must be 'real' in the sense that a reasonable person 'would not brush [it] aside
as far-fetched': see Lord Reid in *Overseas Tankship (UK) Ltd v Miller
Steamship Co Pty (The Wagon Mound No 2)* [1967] 1 AC 617, 643. As the
possible adverse consequences of carelessness increase in seriousness, so will
a lesser degree of likelihood of occurrence suffice to satisfy the test of
reasonable foreseeability." (paras 20–21).

The case involved an incident where a police officer, PC Laurent, shot a member of the public with a police gun to which the authorities had given him access. The police authorities were defendants to the claim, but the officer's action was held to be outside the scope of his duty, thereby excluding vicarious liability. The issue was therefore whether the police authorities were themselves negligent in allowing him access to the gun (see para.18). Two particular features therefore needed consideration: first, the fact that damage was caused by a third party rather than by the defendant (for which, see *Civil Actions Against the Police* (3rd ed.), para.10–013); second, the policy reasons relating to imposing liability on the police (considered *Civil Actions Against the Police* (3rd ed.), paras 10–016 to 10–028).

The proximity issue

10–013   **The general approach** The two proximity factors were both considered by the Privy Council in *Att-Gen v Hartwell* [2004] 1 W.L.R. 1273:

- *Whether the conduct complained of is a positive act or an omission:* The Privy Council held that the case did not fall on the "omission" side of the boundary: the police were not being held liable for failure to carry out their duties properly but for entrusting PC Laurent with a firearm (para.31). This was of "cardinal importance".

- *Whether the damage is caused directly by the defendant or indirectly by a third party whose wrongdoing the defendant had failed to prevent:* Under this heading, Lord Nicholls noted Lord Reid's observations in *Dorset Yacht Co Ltd v Home Office* to the effect that "where human action formed one of the links between the original wrongdoing of the defendant and the plaintiff's loss that action must 'at least have been something very likely to happen . . . '". However, he held that the right approach was that:

    "as with the likelihood that loss will occur, so with the likelihood of wrongful third part intervention causing loss, the degree of likelihood needed to give rise to a duty of care depends on the circumstances . . . The underlying principle is that reasonable foreseeability, as an ingredient of the duty of care, is a broad and flexible standard which is responsive to the infinitely variable circumstances of different cases. The nature and gravity of the damage foreseeable, the likelihood of its occurrence, and the ease or difficulty of eliminating the risk are all matters to be taken into account in the round when deciding whether as a matter of legal policy a duty of care was owed by the defendant to the plaintiff in respect of the damage suffered by him." (para.25)

It was said that this was consistent with the approach of the House of Lords in *Smith v Littlewoods* [1987] A.C. 241.

The policy issue

The "policy limitation" and cases against public authorities

n.57: *W v Home Office* was distinguished in *R. (A) v Secretary of State for the Home Department* [2004] EWHC Admin 1585, at [42], in which Keith J. held that "being required to take care in the administrative implementation of immigration decisions would enhance public confidence in the system, and the administrative implementation of immigration decisions is not an area of human activity in which the fear of being brought to account for one's mistakes is likely to affect performance". He accordingly held that the Secretary of State had a duty to take care in the administrative implementation of immigration decisions (as opposed to decisions which required the exercise of judgment). The case was also distinguished by the Court of Appeal in *Farah v British Airways & The Home Office*, *The Times*, January 26, 2000.

10–019

In the House of Lords judgment in *D v East Berkshire Community NHS Trust* [2005] 2 W.L.R. 993, it was recognised that a local authority may owe a duty of care to a child it suspects of being abused (see, for example, para.30, Lord Bingham; para.106, Lord Rodger; para.125, Lord Brown). However, a majority of the House held that there was no arguable duty to take reasonable care not falsely to accuse the child's *parents* of carrying out that abuse. In a compelling dissent, however, Lord Bingham argued that the matter should be considered in light of the full facts at trial.

10–020

Immunity: the current approach

In *Att-Gen v Hartwell* [2004] 1 W.L.R. 1273, the Privy Council had no difficulty in holding that public policy did not prevent the imposition of a duty on the police in this case, even though it could not be said that the injury was likely. There were two main reasons for this (see paras 31, 32 and 36). First, this was a positive action and not a failure to carry out duties properly. Second, the potential danger posed by loaded guns required particular diligence: "when an article as dangerous as a loaded gun is handed over the class of persons to whom the duty of care is owed is wide and the standard of care required is high".

10–027A

The decision of the Court of Appeal in *Brooks v Commissioner of Police for the Metropolis* was overruled by the House of Lords [2005] 1 W.L.R. 1495. It was held that as a matter of public policy the police generally owed no duty of care to victims or witnesses in respect of their activities when investigating suspected crimes; and that, since the duties of care alleged by the claimant had been inextricably bound up with the investigation of a crime, his claim based

10–028

on those duties should be struck out. Lord Steyn considered that "it would be best for the principle in *Hill* to be reformulated in terms of the absence of a duty of care, rather than a blanket immunity" (para.27). The claim was brought by a friend of Stephen Lawrence, who had witnessed his murder and been attacked himself by the killers, claimed that the police owed him duties to take reasonable steps to protect and support him appropriately, whether as a victim of crime or as an eyewitness, and to give reasonable weight to his account of events and act on it. The House of Lords was satisfied that these duties "could not even arguably be imposed on police officers charged in the public interest with the investigation of a very serious crime and the apprehension of those responsible . . . without potentially undermining the officers' performance of their functions" (*per* Lord Bingham, para.4; see also Lord Nicholls (para.5), Lord Steyn (para.33), and Lord Rodger (para.38)). As a result, the claim was struck out.

10–028A   However, several members of the House of Lords in *Brooks* were of the view that *Hill* should not prevent a proper analysis of the facts in less clear cases. Lord Steyn, having noted (paras 24–27) that *Hill* was not followed in Canada or South Africa and that some of the observations made by Lord Keith are no longer sound, held that "outrageous negligence by the police, unprotected by specific torts . . . could fall beyond the reach of the *Hill* principle" (para.34). Lord Bingham (para.3) and Lord Nicholls (para.6) were willing to contemplate the existence of a duty of care in cases which were not necessarily so extreme as to be termed "outrageous". Accordingly, it is submitted that if there is any doubt, the question of whether a duty of care exists should be examined at trial. (See also *D v East Berkshire Community Health Authority* [2005] 2 W.L.R. 993, in which a majority of the House of Lords held that there could be no duty owed by a health authority investigating allegations of child abuse to the parents of the child. The claim was struck out. Lord Bingham, dissenting, considered that such a duty could arise in appropriate circumstances and preferred to allow the matter to be considered at trial). The judgment of the Privy Council in *Att-Gen v Hartwell* [2004] 1 W.L.R. 1273) suggests that the policy reasons underpinning *Hill*, are less likely to apply to exclude a duty of care where the complaint is of some positive action by the police rather than a failure to carry out their police duties properly.

10–031   In *Brooks v Commissioner of Police* [2005] 1 W.L.R. 1495 Lord Steyn made it clear that, if "assumption of responsibility" is established the *Hill* principle does not apply [29].

Duty of care and statutory discretion

10–038   For a case where a duty of care was imposed on the *implementation* of decisions made under legislation (see *R. (A) v Secretary of State for the Home Department* [2004] EWHC Admin 1585, [42]. Keith J. held that there was nothing in the statutory scheme relating to the grant to asylum seekers of exceptional leave to remain which precluded their having a remedy in negligence for careless failures to provide them with the proper documents to claim benefits (see [18]).

POLICE NEGLIGENCE CLAIMS IN SPECIFIC SITUATIONS

Claimants who assist the police

Police informants

In *X & Y v Chief Constable of Greater Manchester Police* [2004] EWHC QB 764, the police conceded liability in negligence for disclosing the identity of X, an informant, to the defence in the course of a prosecution.

10–066

Failure to protect victims of crime

Case Law in other common law jurisdictions

n.1: The decision that the Canadian police are not immune from failure properly to conduct and ensure co-operation with a special inquiry following a fatal shooting was upheld by the Supreme Court of Canada in *Estate of Odhavji v Woodhouse* [2003] 3 S.C.R. 263.

10–080

Failure to take care in relation to investigations

For a further example of "police investigation immunity" in other common law jurisdictions, see *Cran v New South Wales* [2004] N.S.W.C.A. 92 in which it was held that no duty of care was owed to a claimant who suffers psychiatric harm in prison as a result of his experiences there during an unnecessary prolongation of his imprisonment before trial (See also *New South Wales v Paige* [2002] N.S.W.C.A. 235). In *Sullivan v Moody* (2001) 183 A.L.R. 404, the High Court of Australia held that persons investigating allegations of sexual abuse to a child had no duty to take care to protect suspects, even if they were the child's parents. The same conclusion was reached by the House of Lords in *D v East Berkshire Community Health Authority* [2005] 2 W.L.R. 993.

10–088

DUTY OF CARE AND SPECIAL SITUATIONS

Duties owed to police officers

10–093   In *French v Sussex County Council* [2005] P.I.Q.R. 243, the claimant police officers claimed they were exposed to psychiatric injury as a result of an investigation into a botched raid for which they were blamed but which was in fact the result of negligent corporate failures. Wilkie J. held that, in light of *Frost v Chief Constable of South Yorkshire*, there was no duty of care to protect them from psychiatric injury generally. Nor was there any duty of care arising out of an employer's duty to protect his employees from stress at work, because there was no indication that the claimants were particularly vulnerable to psychiatric injury. Finally, following *Calveley v Chief Constable of Merseyside Police*, there could be no claim for negligence in relation to the pursuit of disciplinary proceedings.

10–094   n.33: See also *Lennon v Commissioner of Police for the Metropolis* [2004] EWCA Civ 130, in which the Commissioner was held to be liable for economic loss suffered by the claimant as a result of following incorrect advice from a personnel executive, on the basis that there had been an "assumption of responsibility".

10–095   In *Donachie v Chief Constable of Greater Manchester* [2004] EWCA Civ 405, the claimant was a police officer who had developed a clinical psychiatric state leading to an acute rise in blood pressure and a stroke after being involved in a stressful police operation. Although the claimant had not in fact suffered physical injury during the operation, he was a "primary victim" and the defendant was liable for his psychiatric injury and its consequences.

CHAPTER 11

Misfeasance and other Civil Actions

MISFEASANCE IN A PUBLIC OFFICE

Introduction

11–002   n.2: For a recent discussion of the elements of the criminal offence of misconduct in a public office, see *Att-Gen's Reference (No.3 of 2003)* [2005] 1 Q.B. 73.

The elements of the tort

11–004   It is now clear that "damage" can include the infringement of a "constitutional" right, such as the right to vote or the right of access to a court, even if it causes no actual loss (*Watkins v Secretary of State for the Home Department* [2005] 2 W.L.R. 1538, paras 48 and 67).

Public officer

General

11–007   n.23a: See also *Ashley v Chief Constable of Sussex Police* [2005] EWHC QB 415, para.55.

Malice

Introduction

11–015   Dobbs J. took the view in *Ashley v Chief Constable of Sussex Police* [2005] EWHC QB 415, at [46]–[50], that the particulars of claim in a misfeasance case must "set out the allegation of dishonesty or bad faith and give particulars". The judgment of the Supreme Court of Canada in *Estate of Odhavji v Woodhouse* [2003] S.C.C. 69, tends to support the view expressed in the main text that bad faith is inherent in either form of malice. The Court held that mere knowledge of harm is insufficient because public officers must be entitled to make decisions adverse to the interests of certain members of the public—there must be "bad faith". However, it seems that this requirement is equivalent to the requirement that "the officer must deliberately engage in conduct that he or she knows to be inconsistent with the obligations of the office" (see [28]).

Knowing or reckless invalidity

The Supreme Court of Canada has recognised that misfeasance may be based on an "improper motive" other than a specific intention to injure the claimant, provided the public officer knows that his conduct is likely to cause such injury: *Estate of Odhavji v Woodhouse* [2003] S.C.C. 69, para.23.   **11–019**

It is clear that malice cannot be founded merely on a claim that an officer "ought to have known" a fact which would take an action outside of his powers: see *Ashley v Chief Constable of Sussex Police* [2005] EWHC QB 415, [64].   **11–020**

Damage

A claim in misfeasance in public office may lie even without proof of loss if the effect was to infringe a "constitutional" right or other right of such importance that the law sees fit to protect it. Thus, in *Watkins v Secretary of State for the Home Department* [2005] 2 W.L.R. 1538, the Court of Appeal held that a claim in misfeasance was made out when prison officers maliciously interfered with a prisoner's correspondence with his solicitor, thereby infringing his constitutional right of access to a court. Laws held that: **11–024**

> "Where a claimant is exposed to economic or material injury by virtue of the public officer's wrongful and malicious act, it will be inherent in his claim that he has suffered quantifiable loss; and he does not have to prove that in causing such loss the public officer has violated some free-standing right which the claimant enjoys. That is one class of case. But the claimant may be adversely affected in a different sense. The wrongful act may have interfered with a right of a kind which the law protects without proof of any loss. In that case, the public officer's interference with the right will complete the tort and no actual damage needs to be shown. This is the second class of case. Its paradigm is the instance where the public officer's unlawful conduct has interfered with a constitutional right." ([67])

See also Brooke L.J. at [48].

DEFAMATION

The nature of the claim

Imputations in police cases

11–056   In *Wood v Chief Constable of the West Midlands Police* [2005] E.M.L.R. 20, the claimant owned a business, Vehicle Salvage Group Limited, with a Mr Hart. A Chief Inspector sent letters to insurance brokers warning them that Mr Hart had been arrested for stealing motor vehicles and that he "now operates under the company name of Vehicle Salvage Group". Such comments were probably lawful. However, the Chief Inspector went on: he stated that his "aim is to inform companies like yourselves of Mr Hart and his attempt to disguise his criminal activities with a veil of legitimacy", urging the recipient to "circulate [Mr Hart's] details in order that he is unable to use a legitimate business front to disguise a criminal venture". The judge left to the jury the question of whether these comments bore a meaning defamatory of the claimant: namely, that, as someone publicly identified as a manager of Vehicle Salvage Group, he was complicit in the commission of a number of offences. The jury found for the claimant and awarded him damages of £45,000.

Defences

Qualified privilege

11–069   **Qualified privilege in police cases** Information released to the press by the police in response to inquiries on a matter of substantial public interest, namely an earlier investigation into suspicious deaths') was held to be subject to qualified privilege (*Oliver v Chief Constable of Northumbria* [2003] EWHC QB 2417. However disclosure in the course of inquiries which goes beyond that required for the detection or prevention of crime or the protection of victims of crime will *not* attract qualified privilege. In *Wood v Chief Constable of the West Midlands Police* [2005] E.M.L.R. 20, a police officer sent notices to members of the public which were held to bear the meaning that the claimant had aided and abetted his business partner, Gary Hart, in criminal offences. Mr Hart had been charged but had not stood trial, and so:

> "particular care was needed. The police had no business, let alone duty, to make statements anticipating that he would be convicted. . . Factual statements about Hart's arrest were one thing. But defamatory statements about [the business] and, as it turned out, about Mr Wood were quite another. These statements. . . did not, as the judge held, sufficiently contribute to

the prevention of crime or the protection of victims to sustain a duty of disclosure." (para.64)

On the facts of the case, therefore, the defence of qualified privilege failed.

Applicability to police cases

For a successful libel claim against a police officer acting in the course of his **11–073** duty, see *Wood v Chief Constable of the West Midlands Police* [2005] E.M.L.R. 20. In contrast, the claim in *Oliver v Chief Constable of Northumbria Police* [2004] EWHC QB 790, was unsuccessful. In that case the claimant was a former police officer who claimed that the publication of a press release concerning a report which he had prepared was defamatory. Gray J. held that the defamatory allegations were justified and that the defendant could not rely on the defence of qualified privilege.

CHAPTER 12

Discrimination Claims

INTRODUCTION

12–006   The scope of justifying less favourable treatment for a reason relating to disability is now much reduced by reason of legislative change and case law (see: s.3A(6); *Collins v Royal National Theatre Board Limited* [2004] I.R.L.R. 395).

12–007   The DDA will be amended by the Disability Discrimination Act 2005 so as to include provision in the DDA similar to that provided for in the RRA by the

RRAA. This is discussed below. In addition, the Equality Bill introduced in the House of Lords on May 18, 2005 (Bill 2-EN) and when enacted this will similarly amend the SDA.

DEFINITIONS OF DISCRIMINATION

Harassment

Two recent cases explore the possibilities for bringing claims under the Protection From Harassment Act 1997, identify the ingredients of the tort and establish that vicarious liability arises in respect of the statutory form of harassment (*Majrowski v Guy's and St Thomas's NHS Trust* [2005] I.R.L.R. 340 and *Banks v Ablex Ltd* [2005] I.R.L.R. 357).   **12–034**

DISCRIMINATION

Meaning of "disability"

Schedule 1 to the DDA will be amended by s.18 of the Disability Discrimination Act 2005 on a date to be appointed by the Secretary of State (see s.20(3)). The result will be to remove the requirement that a mental illness be clinically well-recognised (though it is suggested that this is unlikely in most cases to remove the practical necessity for medical evidence) and to provide that a person with cancer, HIV infection or multiple sclerosis is to be deemed to have a disability.   **12–040**

In *McNicol v Balfour Beatty* [2002] I.R.L.R. 711, the Court of Appeal held that "impairment" bears its ordinary and natural meaning, "[it] may result from illness or it may consist of an illness" (*per* Mummery L.J., para.17). See also *Rugamer v Sony Music Entertainment UK Ltd* [2001] I.R.L.R. 644, in which the EAT held that someone has a physical or mental impairment if they have "something wrong with them physically, or something wrong with them mentally" (and see, *College of Ripon & St John v Hobbs* [2002] I.R.L.R. 185).   **12–041**

n.76. This has been confirmed by the EAT: see *Goodwin v the Patent Office* [1999] I.R.L.R. 4; *Vicary v BT* [1999] I.R.L.R. 680 and see *Leonard v South Derbyshire Chamber of Commerce* [2001] I.R.L.R. 19.   **12–043**

Meaning of disability discrimination

12–051   A new s.21B, inserted into the DDA by the Disability Discrimination Act 2005, will come into force on a date to be appointed. It will make it unlawful for a public authority to discriminate against a disabled person in carrying out its functions. This is likely to cover most police activity which is not already covered by s.19 (save that relating to decisions relating to the institution of criminal proceedings: see s.21C(4)). However, like the equivalent provisions in the RRA, s.21B gives rise to a tort only in relation to discrimination which is not otherwise unlawful. As a result, it will usually be sensible to plead ss.21B and 19 in the alternative. The definitions of "discrimination" for the purposes of s.21B will be set out in s.21D and are similar to those under ss.20 and 21, which are discussed in the main text.

12–060   **Justification** Discrimination under the new s.21B may be justifiable by reference to different conditions, listed under s.21D. They are:

- the treatment, or non-compliance with the duty, is necessary in order not to endanger the health or safety of any person (which may include that of the disabled person);

- the disabled person is incapable of entering into an enforceable agreement, or of giving an informed consent, and for that reason the treatment, or non-compliance with the duty, is reasonable in the particular case;

- in relation to disability-related discrimination, treating the disabled person equally favourably would in the particular case involve substantial extra costs and, having regard to resources, the extra costs in that particular case would be too great;

- the treatment, or non-compliance with the duty, is necessary for the protection of rights and freedoms of other persons;
- the acts of the public authority which give rise to the treatment or failure are a proportionate means of achieving a legitimate aim.

THE UNLAWFUL ACTS

12–081   The decision of the Court of Appeal in *Brooks v Commissioner of Police for the Metropolis* on race discrimination was not appealed to the House of Lords and remains good law ([2005] 1 W.L.R. 1495).

DISCRIMINATION CLAIMS

The general approach and the burden of proof

See *Bahl v Law Society* [2003] I.R.L.R. 640, for a comprehensive consideration of the authorities, approved in the Court of Appeal as "a masterly analysis of the law": [2004] I.R.L.R. 799, para.69.

12–090

The impact of the shift in the burden of proof (under the equivalent provisions applicable in employment cases) was considered in *Igen v Wong* [2005] I.C.R. 931. The Court of Appeal held that a two-stage process is to be undertaken (see para.17). First, the court should consider whether the claimant has proved facts from which it could conclude, by inference if necessary, that an act of discrimination has taken place. At this stage it is to be presumed that there is no adequate explanation for the defendant's behaviour, even if he offers one, but the court can take into account the defendant's evidence if it assists the claimant's case (see paras 20–24). Second, if the claimant is successful on the first stage, the court should go on to consider the defendant's explanation for the act or omission and decide whether he has shown that racial grounds formed *no* part of the reason for his conduct. To avoid a finding of discrimination, the defendants must discharge the burden of proving on the balance of probabilities that race was not a ground for the treatment in question (para.37).

12–093

CHAPTER 13

Judicial Review of Police Decisions

INTRODUCTION

13–003   Significant numbers of judicial review claims now involve challenges under the Human Rights Act. *R. (Green) v PCA* [2004] 1 W.L.R. 725 and *R. (Marper) v Chief Constable of South Yorkshire Police* [2004] 1 W.L.R. 2196 have now been decided by the House of Lords. Other examples include *R. (Laporte) v Chief Constable of Gloucestershire Constabulary* [2005] 1 All E.R. 473 (a challenge to the decision to oblige a coach of protestors to return to London under police escort) and *R. (X) v Chief Constable of West Midlands* [2005] 1 W.L.R. 65 (the disclosure to a prospective employer of details of the claimant's police record).

GENERAL PRINCIPLES OF REVIEW

Public and private law

For an example of a case started as a claim in judicial review, but continued as an ordinary private law claim in the Administrative Court, see *R. (A) v Secretary of State for the Home Department* [2004] EWHC Admin 1585.   13–005

Ground for review

Other developing grounds for judicial review include the unfair frustration of a legitimate expectation (which may be procedural or substantive) conferred on the claimant by some clear promise made by the defendant (see *R. v North and East Devon Health Authority, Ex p. Coughlan* [2001] Q.B. 213) and, in some cases at least, a mistake by the decision maker as to some material and objectively verifiable fact (see *E & R v Secretary of State for the Home Department* [2004] Q.B. 1044; *Begum v London Borough of Tower Hamlets* [2003] 2 A.C. 430, paras 48–49).   13–013

JUDICIAL REVIEW OF POLICING POLICY

Operational policy

The Court of Appeal reiterated its reluctance to circumscribe too closely the discretions accorded to public bodies in *R. (Kent Pharmaceuticals Ltd) v Director of Serious Fraud Office* [2005] 1 All E.R. 449. Kennedy L.J. held at para.20 that the respondent's discretion to give disclosure of documents seized by the SFO to another government department had to be exercised reasonably and in good faith but that it would introduce unnecessary rigidity if the court were to give further guidance on how that discretion should be exercised.   13–040A

PROCEDURE

Applications for permission

Time limits

13–093   The Court of Appeal has confirmed that the requirement for promptness over and above the three-month time limit remains, unless and until it is declared incompatible with Art.6 of the Convention. (*R. (Young) v Oxford City Council* [2002] EWCA Civ 990. And see *Lam v United Kingdom* ECHR judgment of July 5, 2001).)

The determination of the application for permission

13–101   If the claimant is refused permission, the defendant will usually be entitled to the costs of his acknowledgment of service (*R. (Leach) v Commissioner for Local Administration* [2001] 4 P.L.R. 28), but will not usually be entitled to the costs of his attendance at any permission hearing (because such attendance is not required: see *R. (Mount Cook Land Limited) v Westminster City Council* [2003] EWCA Civ 1346). If the Claimant is granted permission, costs will be in the case unless the court orders otherwise (*Practice Note (Administrative Court)* [2004] 2 All E.R. 994).

CHAPTER 14

Damages

DAMAGES IN GENERAL

Types of damages

The basic classification

14-016 Aggravated damages can also, of course, overlap with basic damages as both provide for compensation for injury to feelings. Thus, in *Richardson v Howie* [2004] EWCA Civ 1127, the Court of Appeal held that compensation for injury to feelings caused by the malice or other motive behind a battery should fall within ordinary general damages.

Aggravated damages

14-025 It has now been held that aggravated damages are not appropriate in assault and battery cases, either. As in *AB v South West Water Services* [1993] Q.B. 507, the Court of Appeal took the view in *Richardson v Howie* [2004] EWCA Civ 1127 that general compensatory damages were sufficient. However, unlike in *AB*, it was accepted that the claimant should be compensated for injury to feelings, anger and indignation; it just should not be called "aggravated damages". It may be that this is a step towards the reorganisation sought by the Law Commission in its report on *Aggravated, Exemplary and Restitutionary Damages* whereby there would be only two sorts of damages: a compensatory limb and a punitive limb.

14-028 It appears from the Court of Appeal decision in *Watkins v Secretary of State for the Home Department* [2005] 2 W.L.R. 1538, para.54, that the guidance levels for aggravated and exemplary damages suggested in *Thompson v Commissioner of Police for the Metropolis* apply only to juries. In that case, the Court held that it was open to a judge sitting alone to make an award of exemplary damages below the £5,000 minimum suggested in *Thompson* (see paras 57, 61, and 65).

14-029 See now, however, *Richardson v Howie* [2004] EWCA Civ 1127, which states that in assault and battery cases, at least, injury to feelings should normally be characterised as basic rather than aggravated damages.

Exemplary damages

14-030 **Introduction** Sedley L.J. suggested in *Borders (UK) Ltd and others v Commissioner of Police for the Metropolis and another* [2005] EWCA Civ 197 that the second type of exemplary damages (to prevent calculated profiteering) might be more attractively theorised as restitutionary damages to prevent unjust enrichment, and should therefore be seen as part of basic damages. At [26] he said:

"While such prediction is not a source of present law, it helps to bring the two theories into a single frame by suggesting (as Lord Scott suggested in *Kuddus*) that a modern enhanced compensatory regime is capable of sub-suming the need for punitive awards. When one recalls the rationale of the second category of exemplary damages is, precisely, the confiscation of prof-its which cannot be got at through the ordinary compensatory mechanisms, this is an attractive synthesis. Exemplary damages fill a moral gap, and it has always been the principal moral objection to that that by handing the penal sum to whoever happens to be the claimant the law hands them a windfall."

(See also Rix L.J. at [40]). Whatever might be the destiny of the second category of exemplary damages, however, it remains difficult to see how the first cate-gory (punishment for oppressive, arbitrary or unconstitutional behaviour by governmental bodies) could be subsumed within the law of restitution. For the present, at least, both types of exemplary damages can still be pursued.

Vicarious liability In *Watkins v Secretary of State for the Home Department* [2004] 4 All E.R. 1158, para.54, Brooke L.J. considered counsel's decision *not* to pursue an award of exemplary damages against the vicariously-liable Home Secretary to be "prudent" in light of Lord Scott's comments in *Kuddus v Chief Constable of Leicestershire Constabulary* [2002] 2 A.C. 122. As a result, however, the point was not decided.   14–037

In an appropriate case, there is nothing preventing a judge sitting without a jury from making an award lower than the £5,000 limit suggested in *Thompson v Commissioner of Police for the Metropolis* and he "need not feel constrained by what Lord Woolf MR said": see *Watkins v Secretary of State for the Home Department*, [2005] 2 W.L.R. 1538, paras 57, 61 and 65.   14–040

The principle that exemplary damages should not be awarded where the defendant has been punished by the criminal law does not necessarily apply to the second type of exemplary damages, where the defendant makes a calcu-lated profit from his wrongful act which goes beyond the basic damages awarded to the claimant. In *Borders (UK) Ltd and others v Commissioner of Police for the Metropolis and another* [2005] EWCA Civ 197, the Court of Appeal held that a quantified sum of exemplary damages representing profit the defendant had made on reselling stolen books was proper, even though he had been convicted for it: see [17], [41], and [46]. The fact that those profits could be recouped at a later date under the criminal confiscation regime (then under the Criminal Justice Act 1988; now under the Proceeds of Crime Act 2002) did not give rise to a danger of double punishment, because that regime only bit on realisable assets and the defendant's realisable assets would be reduced by the exemplary damages awarded in the civil case. (It may well be the case that a confiscation order which has *already* been made could prevent a similar award exemplary damages.) Nor did it matter in that case that the claimants could have claimed the sums they obtained in exemplary damages as compensatory damages under the developing law of restitution: it was   14–041 sufficient that the conditions for an award of exemplary damages were also made out: see [28], [39], [43] and [47].

DAMAGES FOR TRESPASS TO THE PERSON

Assault and battery

14–050 The Court of Appeal has held that injury to feelings caused by the motive lying behind an attack should be compensated within general damages, not aggravated damages. In *Richardson v Howie* [2004] EWCA Civ 1127, the Court held that:

> "Where there is an assault [the case actually concerned battery, mainly], the victim will be entitled to be compensated for any injury to his feelings, including the anger and indignation roused. Those feelings may well also be affected by the malicious or spiteful nature of the attack or the motive of the assailant; if so, then the victim must be properly compensated for that, particularly where the injured feelings have been heightened by the motive or spiteful nature of the attack. In our view, damages which provide such compensation should be characterised and awarded therefore as ordinary general damages which they truly are."

It seems, therefore, that injury to feelings caused by the *actual tort* or by wrongful motives closely connected with it and expressed through it is to be compensated as general damages. It is not clear where this leaves injuries to feelings caused by, say, subsequent connected conduct by the defendant founded on the same motives. It is suggested that these would still have to be compensated by aggravated damages. This decision appears inconsistent with *Gerald v Commissioner of Police*, (*The Times*, June 26, 1998), which does not seem to have been cited.

False imprisonment—general considerations

14–051 n.96: see also the summary of the principles which apply to the award of damages in false imprisonment cases in *McFadzean v Construction, Forestry, Mining and Energy Union* [2004] V.S.C. 289, paras 98–116.

DAMAGES IN DISCRIMINATION CASES

14–081 In *Vento v Chief Constable of West Yorkshire* [2003] I.C.R. 318, para.67, the Court of Appeal considered that aggravated damages could be awarded in addition to basic damages for injury to feelings, holding that "the decision whether or not to award aggravated damages and, if so, in what amount must depend on the particular circumstances of the discrimination and on the way in which the complaint of discrimination has been handled". It could now be argued in the light of *Richardson v Howie* [2004] EWCA Civ 1127, that aggravated damages are likely to be appropriate only where the high-handed or malicious behaviour occurs separately from the discrimination complained of. Thus, aggravated damages might be appropriate where, as the Court of Appeal suggests in *Vento*, a complaint about the discrimination is handled in a high-handed or dismissive fashion; but if the discrimination itself is particularly spiteful or oppressive, that simply makes the injury to feelings more severe and would justify a higher basic award.

CHAPTER 15

Other Remedies

PROPERTY TO WHICH THE POLICE MAKE NO CLAIM

The Police (Property) Act 1897

Applications to the magistrates' court

The Court of Appeal in *Gough v Chief Constable of West Midlands Police* [2004] EWCA Civ 206, *per* Park J. at [18]–[19], re-emphasised the point that the procedures under the Police (Property) Act 1897 should not be used where there is a serious dispute as to who is entitled to the property.

15–056

In *Gough v Chief Constable of West Midlands Police* [2004] EWCA Civ 206, Park J. said, *obiter*, that:

15–058

"it would not be a proper exercise of discretion by the magistrates to refuse to order a return of property to the only known person who is admittedly entitled to possession of it at common law. At least that is so in a case where no-one else claims to be the owner of the property and where there is no realistic possibility of anyone else putting forward such a claim." ([22])

Carnwath L.J. offered no strong view on the point, but Potter L.J. disagreed with Park J., saying at [48]:

"I find it inherently rebarbative that, by means of civil proceedings in detinue based on the superior possessory title of the claimant over property held by the police following seizure in the course of investigating a suspected offence, a person may be entitled to recover and continue to enjoy property even though the court may be satisfied that he is not the true owner and has acquired the property illegally, albeit the true owner is not identifiable. It seems to me that the terms of the 1897 Act are such that, in those circumstances, magistrates may well not be obliged to make an order in favour of such a claimant . . .".

CHAPTER 16

The Human Rights Act

GENERAL PRINCIPLES

The proportionality principle

The Strasbourg doctrine of the "margin of appreciation" does not apply to   **16–027A**
domestic courts because, unlike the Strasbourg court, they are in a position to
understand nuances in national conditions and practices. However, the domestic courts will in appropriate cases allow public authorities a "discretionary
area of judgment", the breadth of which will depend on the circumstances of
the case including the broad subject matter (economic policy, for example, is
likely to attract a wider discretionary area of judgment that judicial procedure),
the gravity and severity of the interference with the claimant's rights (loss of liberty, say, or discrimination on serious grounds are likely to be scrutinised more
carefully than a relatively minor restriction on the use of property), and the
identity of the decision-maker (Parliament will usually be accorded more scope
than those with less democratic accountability): see, for example, *Ghaidan v
Godin-Mendoza* [2004] 2 A.C. 557, especially para.19; *R v DPP, Ex p. Kebilene*
[2000] 2 A.C. 326, at 380; *A v Secretary of State for the Home Department*
[2005] 2 W.L.R. 87, especially para.29. It is suggested that, in most police cases,
the discretionary area of judgment is likely to be narrow. Even in areas where
the court does allow a wide discretionary area of judgment, it cannot abandon
its duty to scrutinise the action or decision in question to ensure that the
requirements of proportionality are met. Lord Nicholls said in *Ghaidan* that:

> "Parliament is charged with the primary responsibility for deciding the best
> way of dealing with social problems . . . The readiness of the court to depart
> from the view of the legislature depends upon the subject matter of the legis-
> lation and of the complaint. National housing policy is a field where the court
> will be less ready to intervene. Parliament has to hold a fair balance between
> the competing interests of tenants and landlords, taking into account broad
> issues of social and economic policy. But, even in such a field, where the alleged
> violation comprises differential treatment based on grounds such as race or sex
> or sexual orientation the court will scrutinise with intensity any reasons said
> to constitute justification. The reasons must be cogent if such differential
> treatment is to be justified . . . In the present case the only suggested ground for
> according different treatment to the survivor of same sex couples and opposite
> sex couples cannot withstand scrutiny." (paras 19–20)

The different elements of the "proportionality principle" may attract differ-   **16–027B**
ent degrees of scrutiny. In the House of Lords' decision in *A v Secretary of State
for the Home Department*, the government's statutory power to impose indefinite detention without charge in the face of the terrorist threat, passed in pursuance of a purported derogation from the right to liberty in Art.5 of the
Convention, was challenged on two broad bases: first, that the government was

wrong to consider that the terrorist threat was so serious as to "threaten the life of the nation" so as to justify a derogation; second, that the measures taken were disproportionate and/or discriminatory in that only foreign nationals could be detained. In relation to the assessment of the *threat*, that is to say the sufficiency and importance of the objective behind the measures, considerable regard was paid to the assessment made by the authorities. Lord Bingham held at [19] that:

> "great weight should be given to the judgment of the Home Secretary, his colleagues and Parliament on this question, because they were called on to exercise a pre-eminently political judgment."

See also Lord Hope, [116] and Lady Hale, [226]. Only Lord Hoffmann was prepared to hold that the government had over-estimated the threat and that there was in truth no "public emergency threatening the life of the nation".

16–027C However, a robust approach was taken to the proportionality of the powers conferred to combat that threat, that is to say whether the measures taken in pursuit of the objective were necessary and rationally connected to it. Lord Bingham said 42 that:

> "the appellants are in my opinion entitled to invite the courts to review, on proportionality grounds, the Derogation Order and the compatibility with the Convention of section 23 [of the Anti-Terrorism, Crime and Security Act 2001] and the courts are not effectively precluded by any doctrine of deference from scrutinising the issues raised ... the function of independent judges charged to interpret and apply the law is universally recognised as a cardinal feature of the modern democratic state, a cornerstone of the rule of law itself." ([42])

The powers were held to be disproportionate and discriminatory, and incompatible with the Convention (see, for example, [73] and [139]).

16–028D A similar approach was taken to stop and search powers conferred in response to the terrorist threat in *R. (Gillan) v Commissioner of Police of the Metropolis* [2005] Q.B. 388, paras 33–35. The Court of Appeal held that the dangers and difficulties caused by the risk of terrorist attack meant that the court will rarely interfere with the authorities' analysis of that risk, but it would scrutinise more closely the proportionality of the application of measures taken to combat it in the particular case. The Terrorism Act 2000 conferred power on the Commissioner to authorise (subject to confirmation by the Secretary of State) random stops and searches in a given area, without requiring any reasonable suspicion that the individual stopped posed any particular danger or concern. The statutory scheme and a long sequence of such authorisations covering the whole Metropolitan Police area were held to be lawful, but the particular application of the power in the circumstances of the case was not (because the court was not satisfied that the police officer in question was using the powers for the purposes of deterring and preventing terrorism). It may be that the Court of Appeal accorded greater deference to the authorities when considering the proportionality of the statutory scheme and the authorisations made under it than is appropriate in light of *A*: see the comments made in a rather confusing passage between [33] and [35]. An appeal to the house of Lords is pending.

The case of *A v Secretary of State for the Home Department* establishes that proportionality is a matter of law (or, at least, mixed fact and law) which can be challenged on appeal (see [44]).

16–028E

THE OPERATION OF THE HUMAN RIGHTS ACT 1998

Statutory construction under section 3

General principles

The House of Lords has warned against a too "literalistic" approach to the s.3 obligation: it may be necessary under section 3 actually to *change* the meaning of the statute, provided the new meaning is not inconsistent with a fundamental feature of the legislation. In *Ghaidan v Godin-Mendoza* [2004] 2 A.C. 557, paras 27–34, Lord Nicholls recognised that the courts were still feeling their way forward, but considered the effect of s.3 in detail:

16–033

> "the interpretative obligation decreed by section 3 is of an unusual and far-reaching character. Section 3 may require a court to depart from the unambiguous meaning the legislation would otherwise bear ... Section 3 may require the court to depart from this legislative intention, that is, depart from the intention of the Parliament which enacted the legislation ...
>
> "it becomes impossible to suppose that Parliament intended [in enacting the HRA] that the operation of section 3 should depend critically upon the particular form of words adopted by the Parliamentary draftsman in the statutory provision under consideration. That would make the application of section 3 something of a semantic lottery ...
>
> "the mere fact that the language under consideration is inconsistent with a Convention-compliant meaning does not of itself make a Convention-compliant interpretation impossible. Section 3 enables language to be interpreted restrictively or expansively. But section 3 goes further than this. It is also apt to require a court to read in words which change the meaning of the enacted legislation, so as to make it Convention-compliant. In other words, the intention of Parliament in enacting section 3 was that, to an extent bounded only by what is "possible", a court can modify the meaning, and hence the effect, of primary and secondary legislation.
>
> "Parliament, however, cannot have intended that in the discharge of this extended interpretative function the courts should adopt a meaning

inconsistent with a fundamental feature of the legislation. That would be to cross the constitutional boundary section 3 seeks to demarcate and preserve. Parliament has retained the right to enact legislation in terms which are not Convention-compliant. The meaning imported by application of section 3 must be compatible with the underlying thrust of the legislation being construed. Words implied must, in the phrase of my noble and learned friend, Lord Rodger of Earlsferry, 'go with the grain of the legislation'. Nor can Parliament have intended that section 3 should require courts to make decisions for which they are not equipped. There may be several ways of making a provision Convention-compliant, and the choice may involve issues calling for legislative deliberation."

Lord Rodger and Lady Hale agreed with Lord Nicholls, while Lord Steyn espoused a similarly broad interpretation (see especially [50] in which Lord Steyn says that "in practical effect there is a strong rebuttable presumption in favour of an interpretation consistent with Convention rights"). In *Ghaidan* it was appropriate to expand the meaning of para.2 of Sch.1 of the Rent Act 1977, which unambiguously extended security of tenure only to the survivor of couples living together "as husband and wife", to include the survivor of homosexual couples living together in a close and stable relationship: see paras 35, 51, 129 and 144.

KEY CONVENTION RIGHTS

The right to life under Article 2

The application of Article 2 to police cases

16–051 Article 2 may also, of course, be violated by lethal force used in an attempt to apprehend a suspect. In the remarkable case of *Makaratzis v Greece* (Judgment of December 20, 2004), police fired at the applicant using pistols and submachine guns. He was an unarmed driver who had driven through a red traffic light and, when pursued, had driven in a highly dangerous fashion, hitting several other vehicles and bursting through five police roadblocks during his pursuit. The Court recognised that "it is only in exceptional circumstances that physical ill-treatment by State officials which does not result in death may disclose a violation of Article 2 of the Convention" (para.51), but Art.2 applied given the real risk of death (para.66). The Court accepted that the "the police could reasonably have considered that there was a need to resort to the use of their weapons in order to immobilise the car and neutralise the threat posed by its driver" (para.66). However, the force used was excessive and uncontrolled by a proper legal framework. It was by this absence of an adequate legislative and administrative framework on the use of firearms and the conduct of such chases that

Greece had breached its Art.2 duty to take positive steps to protect life (paras 71–2).

The prohibition of inhuman or degrading treatment under Article 3

Individuals in detention

The Court has stressed that the State is responsible for any person in detention   16–057
because such a person is in a situation of vulnerability and the authorities have a duty to protect him (*Gültekin v Turkey*, Judgment of May 31, 2005, para.26). The Court requires a strict application of fundamental guarantees, from the moment of deprivation of liberty. These include:

- right to an examination by a doctor of the detainee's choice (in addition to examination by a police doctor);
- access to a lawyer;
- access to a family member.

These guarantees, reinforced by prompt judicial intervention, should lead to the detection and prevention of ill treatment. When a person is in custody or is being arrested force which has not been made strictly necessary by his own conduct diminishes human dignity and is, in principle, an infringement of Art.3 (*Balogh v Hungary*, Judgment of July 20, 2004, para.45).

The application of Article 3 to police cases

For further examples of assaults by the police which were held to constitute   16–062
breaches of Art.3 see *Rivas v France* (Judgment of April 1, 2004—kick to the testicles); *Balogh v Hungary* (Judgment of July 20, 2004—perforated eardrum and bruising to face resulting from slaps and punches) and *Toteva v Bulgaria* (Judgment of May 19, 2004 haematoma resulting from blow and kick).

The right to liberty under Article 5

Introduction

Detention short of arrest might, in some circumstances, be insufficient to consti-   16–066
tute a deprivation of liberty. Thus, the European Commission on Human Rights has held that the detention of a 10-year-old at a police station for questioning for

two hours (*X v Germany* (1981) 4 D.R. 158) and the detention of a man with a disease of the nervous system for two hours (*Guenat v Switzerland* (1995) 81A D.R. 130) were was not within Art.5. In *Austin v Commissioner of Police for the Metropolis* ([2005] EWHC QB 480, at [510], Tugendhat J. expressed the view that temporary detention of members of a crowd for their own protection would not be a deprivation of liberty within the meaning of Art.5(1).

16–069   In order for detention to be justified under Art.5, four conditions must be satisfied:

- the detention must be lawful under domestic law;

- domestic law must be sufficiently accessible to the individual and sufficiently precise to enable him to foresee the consequences of the restriction on his rights;

- domestic law must not be arbitrary (in the sense that it was resorted to in bad faith) or disproportionate;

- the ground for the detention must fall within one or more of Art.5(1)(a) to (f).

(For the first three conditions see *R. v Governor of Brockhill Prison, Ex p. Evans (No.2)* [2001] 2 A.C. 19, 38C–E; *ID v Home Office* [2005] EWCA Civ 38, [96].)

Domestic Article 5 cases

16–089A   There have been some domestic decisions on the applicability of Art.5 to measures taken by the police which affect a person's liberty. The courts have drawn a distinction between arrest, which always attracts the protection of Art.5, and "the exercise of police powers that fall short of arrest but none the less prevent an individual doing what he or she likes, [which fall] into a grey area" (see *R. (Gillan) v Commissioner of Police of the Metropolis* [2005] Q.B. 388, para.37). In that case, the Court of Appeal held *obiter* that short detention pursuant to stop and search powers does not engage Art.5 (paras 45–46), while the Divisional Court has held that the use of reasonable force to detain someone to prevent an immediately apprehended breach of the peace was "scarcely detention within the scope of Article 5" (see *R. (Laporte) v Chief Constable of Gloucestershire Police* [2004] 2 All E.R. 874, para.46). In *Austin v Commissioner of Police for the Metropolis* [2005] EWHC QB 480, [72], Tugendhat J. held that the necessity of a particular restriction on liberty is a factor which may take it outside of the scope of Art.5(1) altogether. However, in that case, it was held that the confinement of a group of people in Oxford Circus for several hours was a "deprivation of liberty" within the meaning of Art.5. He went on to hold that the detention was justified under Art.5(1)(c) because the police had reasonable grounds suspect that a breach of the peace was about to be committed by the claimants ([517] to [535]).

Fair trial guarantees under Article 6

The application of Article 6 to police cases

Police officers, of course, have procedural rights in relation to disciplinary pro-   16–095
ceedings under the relevant regulations (see Ch.2, above). However, they are
not entitled to the protection of Art.6. The High Court has held that police
disciplinary proceedings do not amount to a "criminal charge" (*Amis v
Commissioner of Police of the Metropolis* [2004] EWHC QB 683. Moreover, it
is reasonably clear from Strasbourg authority that police disciplinary proceedings fall outside the scope of Art.6 altogether (see *Sygounis v Greece* (1994)
78–A DR 71 and *Pellegrin v France* (2001) 31 E.H.R.R. 26).

Freedom of thought, conscience and religion under Article 9

General principles

It appears that the question as to whether a belief is worthy of protection under   16–108
Art.9 may depend on its effects. The House of Lords held in *R. (Williamson) v
Secretary of State for Education and Employment* [2005] 2 W.L.R. 590, that people are entitled to *hold* such beliefs as they like provided they are not fictitious or
capricious. However, when that belief impacts in some way on others, only those
which are consistent with basic standards of human dignity or integrity and pos-
sess an adequate degree of seriousness and importance will qualify for protection
under Art.9(1). Thus, a parent's request to a school to administer corporal punishment to his child was protected, provided it would not "significantly impair
[that] child's physical or moral integrity". Nonetheless, the prohibition on such
punishment in schools was justified under Art.9(2).

Freedom from discrimination in relation to Convention rights under Article 14

Proving discrimination

When considering whether discrimination is established under Art.14 the court   16–127
should take a simple and non-technical approach. Article 14 applies if the
alleged discrimination is in connection with a Convention right and on a
ground stated in Art.14. If this is the case, the essential question for the court is
whether the difference in treatment can withstand scrutiny (see *R. (Carson) v
Secretary of State for Work and Pensions* [2005] 2 W.L.R. 1369—disapproving
the "four questions" formulated in *Wandsworth LBC v Michalak* [2003] 1

W.L.R. 617, para.20). A distinction is to be drawn between grounds of discrimination which appear to offend respect due to the individual (for example, sex or race), where severe scrutiny is called for and those which merely required some rational justification.

REMEDIES UNDER THE HUMAN RIGHTS ACT

Introduction

Damages under the HRA

16–142   The House of Lords has held that domestic courts should look to awards made by the European Court of Human Rights in deciding whether to award damages and, if so, how much. In *R. (Greenfield) v Secretary of State for the Home Department* [2005] 1 W.L.R. 673, paras 18–19, Lord Bingham disapproved the suggestions made in the cases cited in *Civil Actions Against the Police* (3rd ed.), and held that English courts should not readily apply domestic scales of damages or make comparisons with awards made for discrimination or other torts:

> "courts in this country should look to Strasbourg and not to domestic precedents . . . The [Strasbourg] court routinely describes its awards as equitable, which I take to mean that they are not precisely calculated but are judged by the court to be fair in the individual case. Judges in England and Wales must also make a similar judgment in the case before them. They are not inflexibly bound by Strasbourg awards in what may be different cases. But they should not aim to be significantly more or less generous than the court might be expected to be, in a case where it was willing to make an award at all."

APPENDIX 1

POLICE AND CRIMINAL EVIDENCE ACT 1984

CHAPTER 60

[*Note:* this Appendix *only* includes the sections and sub-sections of the Police and Criminal Evidence Act 1984 which have been amended since the Third Edition of *Civil Actions Against the Police* (up to date as at September 1, 2003). Readers will, therefore, need to use Appendix 1 in the Third Edition to see the unamended sections. The Supplement amendments also have related notes explaining the changes, indicated by [1], [2], etc. in the text.]

PART I

POWERS TO STOP AND SEARCH

s 1 Power of constable to stop and search persons, vehicles etc

(2)   Subject to subsection (3) to (5) below, a constable—   App–002

   (a)   may search—

     (i)   any person or vehicle;

     (ii)   anything which is in or on a vehicle,

for stolen or prohibited articles[, any article to which subsection (8A) below applies or any firework to which subsection (8B) below applies];[1] and

   (b)   may detain a person or vehicle for the purpose of such a search.

(3)   This section does not give a constable power to search a person or vehicle or anything in or on a vehicle unless he has reasonable grounds for suspecting that he will find stolen or prohibited articles[, any article to which subsection (8A) below applies or any firework to which subsection (8B) below applies.][2]

(6)   If in the course of such a search a constable discovers an article which he has reasonable grounds for suspecting to be a stolen or prohibited article[, an article to which subsection (8A) below applies or a firework to which subsection (8B) below applies], he may seize it.[3]

(8)   The offences to which subsection (7)(b)(i) above applies are—

(a)   burglary;
(b)   theft;
(c)   offences under section 12 of the Theft Act 1968 (taking motor vehicle or other conveyance without authority); [. . .]⁴
(d)   offences under section 15 of that Act (obtaining property by deception)[; and
(e)   offences under section 1 of the Criminal Damage Act 1971 (destroying or damaging property)].⁵

[(8B)   This subsection applies to any firework which a person possesses in contravention of a prohibition imposed by fireworks regulations.

(8C)   In this section—

(a)   "firework" shall be construed in accordance with the definition of "fireworks" in section 1(1) of the Fireworks Act 2003; and
(b)   "fireworks regulations" has the same meaning as in that Act.]⁶

NOTES

¹ Words substituted by Serious Organised Crime and Police Act 2005 (c.15), s.115(1), (2); amendment in force July 1, 2005.
² Words substituted by Serious Organised Crime and Police Act 2005 (c.15), s.115(1), (3); amendment in force July 1, 2005.
³ Words substituted by Serious Organised Crime and Police Act 2005 (c.15), s.115(1), (4); amendment in force July 1, 2005.
⁴ Word repealed by Criminal Justice Act 2003 (c.44) s.332, Sch.37, Pt 1; amendment in force January 20, 2004.
⁵ Words inserted by Criminal Justice Act 2003 (c.44) s.1(2); amendment in force January 20, 2004.
⁶ Subsections inserted by Serious Organised Crime and Police Act 2005 (c.15), s.115(1), (5); amendment in force July 1, 2005.

s 4 Road checks

App–005   (4)   An officer may only authorise a road check under subsection (3) above—

(a)   for the purpose specified in subsection (1)(a) above, if he has reasonable grounds—

(i)   for believing that the offence is [an indictable offence];¹ and
(ii)   for suspecting that the person is, or is about to be, in the locality in which vehicles would be stopped if the road check were authorised;

(b)   for the purpose specified in subsection (1)(b) above, if he has reasonable grounds for believing that the offence is [an indictable offence];²
(c)   for the purpose specified in subsection (1)(c) above, if he has reasonable grounds—

(i)   for believing that the offence would be [an indictable offence];³ and
(ii)   for suspecting that the person is, or is about to be, in the locality in which vehicles would be stopped if the road check were authorised;

(d)   for the purpose specified in subsection (1)(d) above, if he has reasonable grounds for suspecting that the person is, or is about to be, in that locality.

(5)   An officer below the rank of superintendent may authorise such a road check if it appears to him that it is required as a matter of urgency for one of the purposes specified in subsection (1) above.

(14) The duties to specify the purposes of a road check imposed by subsections (9) and (13) above include duties to specify any relevant [indictable offence].[4]

NOTES

[1 to 4] Words substituted by Serious Organised Crime and Police Act 2005 (c.15), s.111, Sch.7, Pt 3, para.43(1), (2); amendments in force on a date to be appointed.

s 5 Reports of recorded searches and of road checks

Subsection (1A) repealed by Serious Organised Crime and Police Act 2005 (c.15), ss.59, 174(2), Sch.4, paras 43, 44, Sch.17, Pt 2; amendment in force on a date to be appointed.   **App–006**

s 6 Statutory undertakers etc.

[(1A) Without prejudice to any powers under subsection (1) above, a constable employed [by the [British Transport Police Authority][1]] may stop, detain and search any vehicle before it leaves a goods area which is included in the premises of any successor of the British Railways Board and is used wholly or mainly for the purposes of a relevant undertaking.]   **App–007**

(3)   . . .[2]

(4)   . . .[3]

NOTES

[1]   Words substituted by SI 2004/1573, art.12(1)(e); amendment in force July 1, 2004.
[2 and 3] Subsections (3) and (4) repealed by Energy Act 2004 (c.20), s.197(9), Sch.23, Pt 1: amendment in force April 1 2005.

PART II

POWERS OF ENTRY, SEARCH AND SEIZURE

Search Warrants

s 8 Power of justice of the peace to authorise entry and search of premises

(1)   If on an application made by a constable a justice of the peace is satisfied that there are reasonable grounds for believing—   **App–009**

(a)   that [an indictable offence] has been committed;[1] and

(b)   that there is material on premises [mentioned in subsection (1A) below],[2] which is likely to be of substantial value (whether by itself or together with other material) to the investigation of the offence; and

(c)   that the material is likely to be relevant evidence; and

(d)   that it does not consist of or include items subject to legal privilege, excluded material or special procedure material; and

(e)   that any of the conditions specified in subsection (3) below applies, he may issue a warrant authorising a constable to enter and search the premises [in relation to each set of premises specified in the application],[3]

he may issue a warrant authorising a constable to enter and search the premises.

[(1A) The premises referred to in subsection (1)(b) above are—

(a)   one or more sets of premises specified in the application (in which case the application is for a "specific premises warrant"); or

(b)   any premises occupied or controlled by a person specified in the application, including such sets of premises as are so specified (in which case the application is for an "all premises warrant").][4]

[(1B) If the application is for an all premises warrant, the justice of the peace must also be satisfied—

(a)   that because of the particulars of the offence referred to in paragraph (a) of subsection (1) above, there are reasonable grounds for believing that it is necessary to search premises occupied or controlled by the person in question which are not specified in the application in order to find the material referred to in paragraph (b) of that subsection; and

(b)   that it is not reasonably practicable to specify in the application all the premises which he occupies or controls and which might need to be searched.][5]

[(1C) The warrant may authorise entry to and search of premises on more than one occasion if, on the application, the justice of the peace is satisfied that it is necessary to authorise multiple entries in order to achieve the purpose for which he issues the warrant.][6]

[(1D) If it authorises multiple entries, the number of entries authorised may be unlimited, or limited to a maximum.][7]

[(6) This section applies in relation to a relevant offence (as defined in section 28D(4) of the Immigration Act 1971) as it applies in relation to [an indictable offence][8].]

Notes

[1]   Words substituted by Serious Organised Crime and Police Act 2005 (c.15), s.111, Sch.7, Pt 3, para.43(1), (3): amendment in force on a date to be appointed.

[2]   Words substituted by Serious Organised Crime and Police Act 2005 (c.15), s.113(1), (2), (3)(a); amendment in force on a date to be appointed.

[3]   Words inserted by Serious Organised Crime and Police Act 2005 (c.15), s.113(1), (2), (3)(b); amendment in force on a date to be appointed.

[4 and 5] Subsections inserted by Serious Organised Crime and Police Act 2005 (c.15), s.113(1), (2) (4); amendment in force on a date to be appointed.

[6 and 7] Subsections inserted by Serious Organised Crime and Police Act 2005 (c.15), s.114(1), (2); amendment in force on a date to be appointed.

[8]   Words substituted by Serious Organised Crime and Police Act 2005 (c.15), s.111, Sch.7, Pt 3, para.43(1), (3); amendment in force on a date to be appointed.

s 9 Special provisions as to access

[(2A) Section 4 of the Summary Jurisdiction (Process) Act 1881 (c 24) (which includes provision for the execution of process of English courts in Scotland) and section 29 of the Petty Sessions (Ireland) Act 1851 (c 93) (which makes equivalent provision for execution in Northern Ireland) shall apply to any process issued by a [judge]¹ under Schedule 1 to this Act as it applies to process issued by a magistrates' court under the Magistrates' Courts Act 1980 (c 43).]   **App–010**

NOTE

¹ Words substituted by Courts Act 2003 (c.39) s.65, Sch.4, para.5; amendment in force on a date to be appointed.

s 15 Search warrants—safeguards

(2)   Where a constable applies for any such warrant, it shall be his duty—   **App–016**

  (a)   to state—

    (i)   the ground on which he makes the application; [. . .]¹
    (ii)   the enactment under which the warrant would be issued; [and
    (iii) if the application is for a warrant authorising entry and search on more than one occasion, the ground on which he applies for such a warrant, and whether he seeks a warrant authorising an unlimited number of entries, or (if not) the maximum number of entries desired;]²

  (b)   to specify the [matters set out in subsection (2A) below;]³ and
  (c)   to identify, so far as is practicable, the articles or persons to be sought.

[(2A) The matters which must be specified pursuant to subsection (2)(b) are—

  (a)   if the application is for a specific premises warrant made by virtue of section 8(1A)(a) above or paragraph 12 of Schedule 1 below, each set of premises which it is desired to enter and search;
  (b)   if the application is for an all premises warrant made by virtue of section 8(1A)(b) above or paragraph 12 of Schedule 1 below—

    (i)   as many sets of premises which it is desired to enter and search as it is reasonably practicable to specify;
    (ii)   the person who is in occupation or control of those premises and any others which it is desired to enter and search;
    (iii) why it is necessary to search more premises than those specified under sub-paragraph (i); and
    (iv)   why it is not reasonably practicable to specify all the premises which it is desired to enter and search.]⁴

(5)   A warrant shall authorise an entry on one occasion only [unless it specifies that it authorises multiple entries.]⁵

[(5A) If it specifies that it authorises multiple entries, it must also specify whether the number of entries authorised is unlimited, or limited to a specified maximum.]⁶

(6)   A warrant—

  (a)   shall specify—

    (i)   the name of the person who applies for it;

(ii)   the date on which it is issued;

(iii)   the enactment under which it is issued; and

(iv)   [each set of premises to be searched, or (in the case of an all premises warrant) the person who is in occupation or control of premises to be searched, together with any premises under his occupation or control which can be specified and which are to be searched;][7] and

(b)   shall identify, so far as is practicable, the articles or persons to be sought.

[(7)   Two copies shall be made of a specific premises warrant (see section 8(1A)(a) above) which specifies only one set of premises and does not authorise multiple entries; and as many copies as are reasonably required may be made of any other kind of warrant.][8]

NOTES

[1] Word repealed by Serious Organised Crime and Police Act 2005 (c.15), ss.114(1), (3), (4)(a), 174(2), Sch.17, Pt 2; amendment in force on a date to be appointed.

[2] Words inserted by Serious Organised Crime and Police Act 2005 (c.15), s.114(1), (3), (4)(b) and (c); amendment in force on a date to be appointed.

[3] Words substituted by Serious Organised Crime and Police Act 2005 (c.15), s.113(1), (5), (6); amendment in force on a date to be appointed.

[4] Subsection inserted by Serious Organised Crime and Police Act 2005 (c.15), s.113(1), (5), (7); amendment in force on a date to be appointed.

[5] Words inserted by Serious Organised Crime and Police Act 2005 (c.15), s.114(1), (3), (5); amendment in force on a date to be appointed.

[6] Subsection inserted by Serious Organised Crime and Police Act 2005 (c.15), s.114(1), (3), (6); amendment in force on a date to be appointed.

[7] Words substituted by Serious Organised Crime and Police Act 2005 (c.15), s.113(1), (5), (8); amendment in force on a date to be appointed.

[8] Words substituted by Serious Organised Crime and Police Act 2005 (c.15), s.114(1), (3), (7); amendment in force on a date to be appointed.

s 16 Execution of warrants

App–017

[(2A)   A person so authorised has the same powers as the constable whom he accompanies in respect of—

(a)   the execution of the warrant, and

(b)   the seizure of anything to which the warrant relates.

(2B)   But he may exercise those powers only in the company, and under the supervision, of a constable.][1]

(3)   Entry and search under a warrant must be within [three months][2] from the date of its issue.

[(3A)   If the warrant is an all premises warrant, no premises which are not specified in it may be entered or searched unless a police officer of at least the rank of inspector has in writing authorised them to be entered.][3]

[(3B)   No premises may be entered or searched for the second or any subsequent time under a warrant which authorises multiple entries unless a police officer of at least the rank of inspector has in writing authorises that entry to those premises.][4]

(9)   A constable executing a warrant shall make an endorsement on it stating—

(a) whether the articles or persons sought were found; and
(b) whether any articles were seized, other than articles which were sought; [and,

unless the warrant is a specific premises warrant specifying one set of premises only, he shall do so separately in respect of each set of premises entered and searched, which he shall in each case state in the endorsement.]⁵

(10) *A warrant which—*

(a) *has been executed; or*
(b) *has not been executed within the time authorised for its execution,*

shall be returned—

(i) *if it was issued by a justice of the peace, to the[designated officer for the local justice area in which the justice was acting when he issued the warrant]⁶; and*
(ii) *if it was issued by a judge, to the appropriate officer of the court from which he issued it.*

[(10) A warrant shall be returned to the appropriate person mentioned in subsection (10A) below—

(a) when it has been executed; or
(b) in the case of a specific premises warrant which has not been executed, or an all premises warrant, or any warrant authorising multiple entries, upon the expiry of the period of three months referred to in subsection (3) above or sooner.

(10A) The appropriate person is—

(a) if the warrant was issued by a justice of the peace, the designated officer for the local justice area in which the justice was acting when he issued the warrant;
(b) if it was issued by a judge, the appropriate officer of the court from which he issued it.]⁷

(11) A warrant which is returned under subsection (10) above shall be retained for 12 months from its return—

(a) by the [designated officer for the local justice area]⁷, if it was returned under paragraph (i) of that subsection; and
(b) by the appropriate officer, if it was returned under paragraph (ii).

(12) If during the period for which a warrant is to be retained the occupier of [premises]⁹ to which it relates asks to inspect it, he shall be allowed to do so.

NOTES

¹ Subsections inserted by Criminal Justice Act 2003 (c.44) s.2; amendment in force January 20, 2004.
² Words substituted by Serious Organised Crime and Police Act 2005 (c.15), s.114(1), (8)(a); amendment in force on a date to be appointed.
³ Words inserted by Serious Organised Crime and Police Act 2005 (c.15), s.113(1), (9)(a); amendment in force on a date to be appointed.
⁴ Words inserted by Serious Organised Crime and Police Act 2005 (c.15), s.114(1), (8)(b); amendment in force on a date to be appointed.
⁵ Words inserted by Serious Organised Crime and Police Act 2005 (c.15), s.113(1), (9)(b); amendment in force on a date to be appointed.

[6] In first subsection (10), words substituted by Courts Act 2003 (c.39), s.190(1), Sch.8, para.281(1), (2); amendment in force July 1, 2005.

[7] Subsections substituted by Serious Organised Crime and Police Act 2005 (c.15), s.114(1), (8)(c); amendment in force on a date to be appointed.

[8] Words substituted by Courts Act 2003 (c.39), s.190(1), Sch.8, para.281(1), (3); amendment in force April 1, 2005.

[9] Words substituted by Serious Organised Crime and Police Act 2005 (c.15), s.113(1), (9)(c); amendment in force on a date to be appointed.

Entry and Search Without Search Warrant

s 17 Entry for purpose of arrest etc

App–018

(1) Subject to the following provisions of this section, and without, prejudice to any other enactment, a constable may enter and search any premises for the purpose—

    (a)   of executing—

        (i)   a warrant of arrest issued in connection with or arising out of criminal proceedings; or

        (ii)   a warrant of commitment issued under section 76 of the Magistrates' Courts Act 1980;

    (b)   of arresting a person for an [indictable] offence;[1]

    (c)   of arresting a person for an offence under—

        (i)   section 1 (prohibition of uniforms in connection with political objects) . . . of the Public Order Act 1936;

        (ii)   any enactment contained in section 6 to 8 or 10 of the Criminal Law Act 1977 (offences relating to entering and remaining on property);

        [(iii)   section 4 of the Public Order Act 1986 (fear or provocation of violence);]

        [(iiia) section 4 (driving etc when under influence of drink or drugs) or 163 (failure to stop when required to do so by constable in uniform) of the Road Traffic Act 1988;

        (iiib) section 27 of the Transport and Works Act 1992 (which relates to offences involving drink or drugs);][2]

        [(iv)   section 76 of the Criminal Justice and Public Order Act 1994 (failure to comply with interim possession order);]

    [(ca) of arresting, in pursuance of section 32(1A) of the Children and Young Persons Act 1969, any child or young person who has been remanded or committed to local authority accommodation under section 23(1) of that Act;

    [(caa) of arresting a person for an offence to which section 61 of the Animal Health Act 1981 applies;][3]

    (cb) of recapturing any person who is, or is deemed for any purpose to be, unlawfully at large while liable to be detained—

        (i)   in a prison, remand centre, young offender institution or secure training centre, or

        (ii)   in pursuance of [section 92 of the Powers of Criminal Courts (Sentencing) Act 2000] (dealing with children and young persons guilty of grave crimes), in any other place;]

(d) of recapturing [any person whatever] who is unlawfully at large and whom he is pursuing; or

(e) of saving life or limb or preventing serious damage to property.

NOTES

[1] Word substituted by Serious Organised Crime and Police Act 2005 (c.15), s.111, Sch.7, Pt 3, para.43(1), (4); amendment in force on a date to be appointed.
[2] Subsections substituted by Serious Organised Crime and Police Act 2005 (c.15), s.111, Sch.7, Pt 4, para.58(a); amendment in force on a date to be appointed.
[3] Subsection inserted by Serious Organised Crime and Police Act 2005 (c.15), s.111, Sch.7, Pt 4, para.58(b); amendment in force on a date to be appointed.

s 18 Entry and search after arrest

(1) Subject to the following provisions of this section, a constable may enter and search any premises occupied or controlled by a person who is under arrest for an [indictable] offence, if he has reasonable grounds for suspecting that there is on the premises evidence, other than items subject to legal privilege, that relates—   **App–019**

(a) to that offence; or
(b) to some other [indictable] offence which is connected with or similar to that offence.[1]

[(5) A constable may conduct a search under subsection (1)—

(a) before [the person is taken] to a police station or released on bail under section 30A, and
(b) without obtaining an authorisation under subsection (4),

if the condition in subsection (5A) is satisfied.

(5A) The condition is that the presence of the person at a place (other than a police station) is necessary for the effective investigation of the offence.][2]

NOTES

[1] Words substituted by Serious Organised Crime and Police Act 2005 (c.15), s.111, Sch.7, Pt 3, para.43(1), (5); amendment in force on a date to be appointed.
[2] Subsections substituted by Criminal Justice Act 2003 (c.44), s.12, Sch.1 paras 1, 2; amendment in force January 20, 2004.

Seizure etc.

. . .

s 21 Access and copying

[(9) The references to a constable in subsections (1), (2), (3)(a) and (5) include a person authorised under section 16(2) to accompany a constable executing a warrant.][1]   **App–022**

NOTE

[1] Subsection inserted by Criminal Justice Act 2003 (c.44), s.12, Sch.1, paras 1, 3; amendment in force January 20, 2004.

s 22 Retention

App–023   [(7)   The reference in subsection (1) to anything seized by a constable includes anything seized by a person authorised under section 16(2) to accompany a constable executing a warrant.][1]

NOTE

[1] Subsection inserted by Criminal Justice Act 2003 (c.44), Sch.1, para.4; amendment in force January 20, 2004.

Part II—Supplementary

s 23 Meaning of "premises" etc

App–024   In this Act—

"premises" includes any place and, in particular, includes—

(a)   any vehicle, vessel, aircraft or hovercraft;
(b)   any offshore installation;
[(ba) any renewable energy installation;][1]
(c)   any tent or movable structure; [. . .][2]

"offshore installation" has the meaning given to it by section 1 of the Mineral Workings (Offshore Installations) Act 1971;

["renewable energy installation" has the same meaning as in Chapter 2 of Part 2 of the Energy Act 2004].[3]

NOTES

[1] Words substituted by Energy Act 2004 (c.20), s.103(2)(a); amendment in force October 5, 2004.
[2] Words repealed by Energy Act 2004 (c.20), Sch.23, Pt 1; amendment in force October 5, 2004.
[3] Definition inserted by Energy Act 2004 (c.20), s.103(2)(b); amendment in force October 5, 2004.

PART III

ARREST

[s 24 Arrest without warrant: constables

(1)   A constable may arrest without a warrant—   App—025

    (a)   anyone who is about to commit an offence
    (b)   anyone who is in the act of committing an offence;
    (c)   anyone whom he has reasonable grounds for suspecting to be about to commit an offence;
    (d)   anyone whom he has reasonable grounds for suspecting to be committing an offence.

(2)   If a constable has reasonable grounds for suspecting that an offence has been committed, he may arrest without a warrant anyone whom he has reasonable grounds to suspect of being guilty of it.

(3)   If an offence has been committed, a constable may arrest without a warrant—

    (a)   anyone who is guilty of the offence;
    (b)   anyone whom he has reasonable grounds for suspecting to be guilty of it.

(4)   But the power of summary arrest conferred by subsection (1), (2), or (3) is exercisable only if the constable has reasonable grounds for believing that for any of the reasons mentioned in subsection (5) it is necessary to arrest the person in question.

(5)   The reasons are—

    (a)   to enable the name of the person in question to be ascertained) in the case where the constable does not know, and cannot readily ascertain, the person's name, or has reasonable grounds for doubting whether a name given by the person as his name is his real name);
    (b)   correspondingly as regards the person's address;
    (c)   to prevent the person in question—

        (i)   causing physical injury to himself or any other person;
        (ii)   suffering physical injury;
        (iii)   causing loss or damage to property;
        (iv)   committing an offence against public decency (subject to subsection (6)); or
        (v)   causing an unlawful obstruction of the highway;

    (d)   to protect a child or other vulnerable person from the person in question;
    (e)   to allow the prompt and effective investigation of the offence or of the conduct of the person in question;
    (f)   to prevent any prosecution for the offence from being hindered by the disappearance of the person in question.

(6)   Subsection (5)(c)(iv) applies only where members of the public going about their normal business cannot reasonably be expected to avoid the person in question.][1]

NOTE

[1] Section substituted in full by Serious Organised Crime and Police Act 2005 (c.15), s.110(1); amendment in force on a date to be appointed.

[s 24A Arrest without warrant: other persons

App–025A
(1) A person other than a constable may arrest without a warrant—

(a) anyone who is in the act of committing an indictable offence;
(b) anyone whom he has reasonable grounds for suspecting to be about to commit an indictable offence.

(2) Where an indictable offence has been committed, a person other than a constable may arrest without a warrant—

(a) anyone who is guilty of the offence;
(b) anyone whom he has reasonable grounds for suspecting to be guilty of it.

(3) But the power of summary arrest conferred by subsection (1) or (2) is exercisable only if—

(a) the person making the arrest has reasonable grounds for believing that for any of the reasons mentioned in subsection (4) it is necessary to arrest the person in question; and
(b) it appears to the person making the arrest that it is not reasonably practicable for a constable to make it instead.

(4) The reasons are to prevent the person in question—

(i) causing physical injury to himself or any other person;
(ii) suffering physical injury;
(iii) causing loss or damage to property; or
(iv) making off before a constable can assume responsibility for him.][1]

NOTE

[1] Section inserted by Serious Organised Crime and Police Act 2005 (c.15), s.110(1); amendment in force on a date to be appointed.

s 25 General arrest conditions

App–026 Section repealed by Serious Organised Crime and Police Act 2005 (c.15), ss.110(2), 174(2), Sch.17, Pt 2; amendment in force on a date to be appointed.

s 30 Arrest elsewhere than at police station

App–031
[(1) Subsection (1A) applies where a person is, at any place other than a police station—

(a) arrested by a constable for an offence, or
(b) taken into custody by a constable after being arrested for an offence by a person other than a constable.

(1A) The person must be taken by a constable to a police station as soon as practicable after the arrest.

(1B) Subsection (1A) has effect subject to section 30A (release on bail) and subsection (7) (release without bail).]¹

(2) Subject to subsections (3) and (5) below, the police station to which an arrested person is taken under [subsection (1A)]² above shall be a designated police station.

[(7) A person arrested by a constable at any place other than a police station must be released without bail if the condition in subsection (7A) is satisfied.

(7A) The condition is that, at any time before the person arrested reaches a police station, a constable is satisfied that there are no grounds for keeping him under arrest or releasing him on bail under section 30A.]³

[(10) Nothing in subsection (1A) or in section 30A prevents a constable delaying taking a person to a police station or releasing him on bail if the condition in subsection (10A) is satisfied.

(10A) The condition is that the presence of the person at a place (other than a police station) is necessary in order to carry out such investigations as it is reasonable to carry out immediately.

(11) Where there is any such delay the reasons for the delay much be recorded when the person first arrives at the police station or (as the case may be) is released on bail.]⁴

(12) Nothing in [subsection (1A) or section 30A]⁵ above shall be taken into effect—

(a) paragraphs 16(3) or 18(1) of Schedule 2 to the Immigration Act 1971;
(b) section 34(1) of the Criminal Justice Act 1972; or
[(c) any provision of the Terrorism Act 2000.]

NOTES

¹ Subsections substituted by Criminal Justice Act 2003 (c.44), s.4(1), (2); amendment in force January 20, 2004.
² Words substituted by Criminal Justice Act 2003 (c.44), s.4(1), (3); amendment in force January 20, 2004.
³ Subsections substituted by Criminal Justice Act 2003 (c.44), s.4(1), (4); amendment in force January 20, 2004.
⁴ Subsections substituted by Criminal Justice Act 2003 (c.44) s.4(1), (5); amendment in force January 20, 2004.
⁵ Words substituted by Criminal Justice Act 2003 (c.44) s.4(1), (6); amendment in force January 20, 2004.

[s 30A Bail elsewhere than at police station

(1) A constable may release on bail a person who is arrested or taken into custody in the circumstances mentioned in section 30(1).   **App–031A**

(2) A person may be released on bail under subsection (1) at any time before he arrives at a police station.

(3) A person released on bail under subsection (1) must be required to attend a police station.

(4) No other requirement may be imposed on the person as a condition of bail.

(5)   The police station which the person is required to attend may be any police station.]¹

NOTE

¹ Section inserted by Criminal Justice Act 2003 (c.44), s.4(1), (7); amendment in force January 20, 2004.

[s 30B Bail under section 30A: notices

App–031B

(1)   Where a constable grants bail to a person under section 30A, he must give that person a notice in writing before he is released.

(2)   The notice must state—

   (a)   the offence for which he was arrested, and
   (b)   the ground on which he was arrested.

(3)   The notice must inform him that he is required to attend a police station.

(4)   It may also specify the police station which he is required to attend and the time when he is required to attend.

(5)   If the notice does not include the information mentioned in subsection (4), the person must subsequently be given a further notice in writing which contains that information.

(6)   The person may be required to attend a different police station from that specified in the notice under subsection (1) or (5) or to attend at a different time.

(7)   He must be given notice in writing of any such change as is mentioned in subsection (6) but more than one such notice may be given to him.]¹

NOTE

¹ Section inserted by Criminal Justice Act 2003 (c.44), s.4(1), (7); amendment in force January 20, 2004.

[s 30C Bail under section 30A: supplemental

App–031C

(1)   A person who has been required to attend a police station is not required to do so if he is given notice in writing that his attendance is no longer required.

(2)   If a person is required to attend a police station which is not a designated police station he must be—

   (a)   released, or
   (b)   taken to a designated police station,

not more than six hours after his arrival.

(3)   Nothing in the Bail Act 1976 applies in relation to bail under section 30A.

(4)   Nothing in section 30A or 30B or in this section prevents the re-arrest without a warrant of a person released on bail under section 30A if new evidence justifying a further arrest has come to light since his release.]¹

NOTE

[1] Section inserted by Criminal Justice Act 2003 (c.44), s.4(1), (7); amendment in force January 20, 2004.

[s 30D Failure to answer to bail under section 30A

(1)   A constable may arrest without a warrant a person who—   App—031D

(a)   has been released on bail under section 30A subject to a requirement to attend a specified police station, but
(b)   fails to attend the police station at the specified time.

(2)   A person arrested under subsection (1) must be taken to a police station (which may be the specified police station or any other police station) as soon as practicable after the arrest.

(3)   In subsection (1), "specified" means specified in a notice under subsection (1) or (5) of section 30B or, if notice of change has been given under subsection (7) of that section, in that notice.

(4)   For the purposes of—

(a)   section 30 (subject to the obligation in subsection (2)), and
(b)   section 31,

an arrest under this section is to be treated as an arrest for an offence.][1]

NOTE

[1] Section inserted by Criminal Justice Act 2003 (c.44), s.4(1), (7); amendment in force January 20, 2004.

s 32 Search upon arrest

(2)   Subject to subsections (3) to (5) below, a constable shall also have power in any   App—033
such case—

(a)   to search the arrested person for anything—

(i)   which he might use to assist him to escape from lawful custody; or
(ii)   which might be evidence relating to an offence; and

(b)   [if the offence for which he has been arrested is an indictable offence, to enter and search any premises in which he was when arrested or immediately before he was arrested for evidence relating to that offence.][1]

NOTE

[1] Words substituted by Serious Organised Crime and Police Act 2005 (c.15), s.111, Sch.7, Pt 3, para.43(1), (6); amendment in force on a date to be appointed.

PART **IV**

DETENTION

Detention—Conditions and Duration

s 34 Limitations on police detention

App–034   (6)   For the purposes of this Part of this Act a person arrested under [section 6D of the Road Traffic Act 1988][1] [or section 30(2) of the Transport and Works Act 1992 (c 42)] is arrested for an offence.

[(7)   For the purposes of this Part a person who—

(a)   attends a police station to answer to bail granted under section 30A
(b)   returns to a police station to answer to bail granted under this Part, or
(c)   is arrested under section 30D or 46A,

is to be treated as arrested for an offence and that offence is the offence in connection with which he was granted bail.][2]

NOTES

[1] Words substituted by Railways and Transport Safety Act 2003 (c.20), s.107, Sch.7, para.12; amendment in force March 30, 2004.
[2] Words substituted by Criminal Justice Act 2003 (c.44), s.12, Sch.1, paras 1, 5; amendment in force January 20, 2004.

s 35 Designated police stations

App–035   (1)   The chief officer of police for each police area shall designate the police stations in his area which, subject to [sections 30(3) and (5), 30A(5) and 30D(2)][1], are to be the stations in that area to be used for the purpose of detaining arrested persons.

NOTE

[1] Words substituted by Criminal Justice Act 2003 (c.44), s.12, Sch.1, paras 1, 6; amendment in force January 20, 2004.

s 36 Custody officers at police stations

App–036   [(3)   No person may be appointed a custody officer unless—

(a)   he is a police officer of at least the rank of sergeant; or
(b)   he is a staff custody officer.][1]

(5)   Subject to the following provisions of this section and to section 39(2) below, none of the functions of a custody officer in relation to a person shall be per-

formed by [an individual]² who at the time when the function falls to be performed is involved in the investigation of an offence for which that person is in police detention at that time.

(7) Where an arrested person is taken to a police station which is not a designated police station, the functions in relation to him which at a designated police station would be the functions of a custody officer shall be performed—

    (a) by an officer [or a staff custody officer]³ who is not involved in the investigation of an offence for which he is in police detention, if [such a person]⁴ is readily available; and

    (b) if no [such person]⁵ is readily available, by the officer who took him to the station or any other officer.

[(7A) Subject to subsection (7B), subsection (7) applies where a person attends a police station which is not a designated station to answer to bail granted under section 30A as it applies where a person is taken to such a station.

(7B) Where subsection (7) applies because of subsection (7A), the reference in subsection (7)(b) to the officer who took him to the station is to be read as a reference to the officer who granted him bail.]⁶

(8) References to a custody officer in [section 34 above or in]⁷ the following provisions of this Act include references to [a person]⁸ other than a custody officer who is performing the functions of a custody officer by virtue of subsection (4) or (7) above.

[(11) In this section, "staff custody officer" means a person who has been designated as such under section 38 of the Police Reform Act 2002.]⁹

Notes

¹ Words substituted by Serious Organised Crime and Police Act 2005 (c.15), s.121(1), (2); amendment in force on a date to be appointed.
² Words substituted by Serious Organised Crime and Police Act 2005 (c.15), s.121(1), (3); amendment in force on a date to be appointed.
³ Words inserted by Serious Organised Crime and Police Act 2005 (c.15), s.121(1), (4)(a)(i); amendment in force on a date to be appointed.
⁴ Words substituted by Serious Organised Crime and Police Act 2005 (c.15), s.121(1), (4)(a)(ii); amendment in force on a date to be appointed.
⁵ Words substituted by Serious Organised Crime and Police Act 2005 (c.15), s.121(1), (4)(b); amendment in force on a date to be appointed.
⁶ Subsections inserted by Criminal Justice Act 2003 (c.44), s.12, Sch.1 Paras 1, 7; amendment in force January 20, 2004.
⁷ Words inserted by Serious Organised Crime and Police Act 2005 (c.15), s.121(1), (5)(a); amendment in force on a date to be appointed.
⁸ Words substituted by Serious Organised Crime and Police Act 2005 (c.15), s.121(1), (5)(b); amendment in force on a date to be appointed.
⁹ Subsection inserted by Serious Organised Crime and Police Act 2005 (c.15), s.121(1), (6); amendment in force on a date to be appointed.

s 37 Duties of custody officer before charge

(7) Subject to section 41(7) below, if the custody officer determines that he has before him sufficient evidence to charge the person arrested with the offence for which he was arrested, the person arrested—

                  App–037

[(a) shall be released without charge and on bail for the purpose of enabling the Director of Public Prosecutions to make a decision under section 37B below;

(b) shall be released without charge and on bail but not for that purpose;

(c) shall be released without charge and without bail, or

(d) shall be charged.]¹

[(7A) The decision as to how a person is to be dealt with under subsection (7) above shall be that of the custody officer.

(7B) Where a person is released under subsection (7)(a) above, it shall be the duty of the custody officer to inform him that he is being released to enable the Director of Public Prosecutions to make a decision under section 37B below.]²

(8) Where—

(a) a person is released under subsection (7)(b)[or (c)]³ above; and

(b) at the time of his release a decision whether he should be prosecuted for the offence for which he was arrested has not been taken,

it shall be the duty of the custody officer so to inform him.

[(8A) Subsection (8B) applies if the offence for which the person is arrested is one in relation to which a sample could be taken under section 63B below and the custody officer—

(a) is required in pursuance of subsection (2) above to release the person arrested and decides to release him on bail, or

(b) decides in pursuance of subsection (7)(a) or (b) above to release the person without charge and on bail.

(8B) The detention of the person may be continued to enable a sample to be taken under section 63B, but this subsection does not permit a person to be detained for a period of more than 24 hours after the relevant time.]⁴

NOTES

¹ Words substituted by Criminal Justice Act 2003 (c.44), s.28, Sch.2, paras 1, 2(1), (2); amendment in force January 29, 2004.
² Subsections inserted by Criminal Justice Act 2003 (c.44), s.28, Sch.2, paras 1, 2(1), (3); amendment in force January 29, 2004.
³ Words inserted by Criminal Justice Act 2003 (c.44), s.28, Sch.2, paras 1, 2(1), (4); amendment in force January 29, 2004.
⁴ Subsections inserted by the Drugs Act 2005 (c.17), s.23(1), Sch.1, paras 1, 2; amendment in force on a date to be appointed.

[s 37A Guidance

App–037A (1) The Director of Public Prosecutions may issue guidance—

(a) for the purpose of enabling custody officers to decide how persons should be dealt with under section 37(7) above or 37C(2) below, and

(b) as to the information to be sent to the Director of Public Prosecutions under section 37B(1) below.

(2) The Director of Public Prosecutions may from time to time revise guidance issued under this section.

(3) Custody officers are to have regard to guidance under this section in deciding how persons should be dealt with under section 37(7) above or 37C(2) below.

(4) A report under section 9 of the Prosecution of Offences Act 1985 (report by DPP to Attorney General) must set out the provisions of any guidance issued, and any revisions to guidance made, in the year to which the report relates.

(5) The Director of Public Prosecutions must publish in such manner as he thinks fit—

(a) any guidance issued under this section, and
(b) any revisions made to such guidance.

(6) Guidance under this section may make different provision for different cases, circumstances or areas.]¹

NOTE

¹ Section inserted by Criminal Justice Act 2003 (c.44), s.28, Sch.2, paras 1, 3; amendment in force January 29, 2004.

[s 37B Consultation with the Director of Public Prosecutions

(1) Where a person is released on bail under section 37(7)(a) above, an officer involved in the investigation of the offence shall, as soon as is practicable, send to the Director of Public Prosecutions such information as may be specified in guidance under section 37A above.   App–037B

(2) The Director of Public Prosecutions shall decide whether there is sufficient evidence to charge the person with an offence.

(3) If he decides that there is sufficient evidence to charge the person with an offence, he shall decide—

(a) whether or not the person should be charged and, if so, the offence with which he should be charged, and
(b) whether or not the person should be given a caution and, if so, the offence in respect of which he should be given a caution.

(4) The Director of Public Prosecutions shall give written notice of his decision to an officer involved in the investigation of the offence.

(5) If his decision is—

(a) that there is not sufficient evidence to charge the person with an offence, or
(b) that there is sufficient evidence to charge the person with an offence but that the person should not be charged with an offence or given a caution in respect of an offence,

a custody officer shall give the person notice in writing that he is not to be prosecuted.

(6) If the decision of the Director of Public Prosecutions is that the person should be charged with an offence, or given a caution in respect of an offence, the person shall be charged or cautioned accordingly.

(7) But if his decision is that the person should be given a caution in respect of the offence and it proves not to be possible to give the person such a caution, he shall instead be charged with the offence.

(8) For the purposes of this section, a person is to be charged with an offence either—

(a) when he is in police detention after returning to a police station to answer bail or is otherwise in police detention at a police station, or
(b) in accordance with section 29 of the Criminal Justice Act 2003.

(9) In this section "caution" includes—

(a) a conditional caution within the meaning of Part 3 of the Criminal Justice Act 2003, and
(b) a warning or reprimand under section 65 of the Crime and Disorder Act 1998.][1]

NOTE

[1] Section inserted by Criminal Justice Act 2003 (c.44), s.28, Sch.2, paras 1, 3; subss.(1) to (7) and (9)(b) in force January 29, 2004; subs.(9)(a) in force July 3, 2004; subs.(8) in force on a date to be appointed.

[s 37C Breach of bail following release under section 37(7)(a)

App–037C (1) This section applies where—

(a) a person released on bail under section 37(7)(a) above or subsection (2)(b) below is arrested under section 46A below in respect of that bail, and
(b) at the time of his detention following that arrest at the police station mentioned in section 46A(2) below, notice under section 37B(4) above has not been given.

(2) The person arrested—

(a) shall be charged, or
(b) shall be released without charge, either on bail or without bail.

(3) The decision as to how a person is to be dealt with under subsection (2) above shall be that of a custody officer.

(4) A person released on bail under subsection (2)(b) above shall be released on bail subject to the same conditions (if any) which applied immediately before his arrest.][1]

NOTE

[1] Section inserted by Criminal Justice Act 2003 (c.44), s.28, Sch.2, paras 1, 3; amendment in force January 29, 2004.

[s 37D Release under section 37(7)(a): further provision

App–037D (1) Where a person is released on bail under section 37(7)(a) or section 37C(2)(b) above, a custody officer may subsequently appoint a different time, or an additional time, at which the person is to attend at the police station to answer bail.

(2) The custody officer shall give the person notice in writing of the exercise of the power under subsection (1).

(3)   The exercise of the power under subsection (1) shall not affect the conditions (if any) to which bail is subject.

(4)   Where a person released on bail under section 37(7)(a) or 37C(2)(b) above returns to a police station to answer bail or is otherwise in police detention at a police station, he may be kept in police detention to enable him to be dealt with in accordance with section 37B or 37C above or to enable the power under subsection (1) above to be exercised.

(5)   If the person is not in a fit state to enable him to be so dealt with or to enable that power to be exercised, he may be kept in police detention until he is.

(6)   Where a person is kept in police detention by virtue of subsection (4) or (5) above, section 37(1) to (3) and (7) above (and section 40(8) below so far as it relates to section 37(1) to (3)) shall not apply to the offence in connection with which he was released on bail under section 37(7)(a) or 37C(2)(b) above.][1]

NOTE

[1] Section inserted by Criminal Justice Act 2003 (c.44), s.28, Sch.2, paras 1, 3; amendment in force January 29, 2004.

s 38 Duties of custody officer after charge

(1)   Where a person arrested for an offence otherwise than under a warrant endorsed for bail is charged with an offence, the custody officer shall[, subject to section 25 of the Criminal Justice and Public Order Act 1994], order his release from police detention, either on bail or without bail, unless—   **App–038**

    (a)   if the person arrested is not an arrested juvenile—

        (i)   his name or address cannot be ascertained or the custody officer has reasonable grounds for doubting whether a name or address furnished by him as his name or address is his real name or address;

        [(ii) the custody officer has reasonable grounds for believing that the person arrested will fail to appear in court to answer to bail;

        (iii) in the case of a person arrested for an imprisonable offence, the custody officer has reasonable grounds for believing that the detention of the person arrested is necessary to prevent him from committing an offence;

        [(iiia) except in a case where (by virtue of subsection (9) of section 63B below) that section does not apply, the custody officer has reasonable grounds for believing that the detention of the person is necessary to enable a sample to be taken from him under that section;][1]

        [(iiia) in a case where a sample may be taken from the person under section 63B below, the custody officer has reasonable grounds for believing that the detention of the person is necessary to enable the sample to be taken from him;][2]

        (iv) in the case of a person arrested for an offence which is not an imprisonable offence, the custody officer has reasonable grounds for believing that the detention of the person arrested is necessary to prevent him from causing physical injury to any other person or from causing loss of or damage to property;

        (v) the custody officer has reasonable grounds for believing that the detention of the person arrested is necessary to prevent him from interfering with the administration of justice or with the investigation of offences or of a particular offence; or

   (vi) the custody officer has reasonable grounds for believing that the detention of the person arrested is necessary for his own protection;]

  (b) if he is an arrested juvenile—

   (i) any of the requirements of paragraph (a) above is satisfied [(but, in the case of paragraph (a)(iiia) above, only if the arrested juvenile has attained the minimum age)];[3] or

   (ii) the custody officer has reasonable grounds for believing that he ought to be detained in his own interests.

[(2A) The custody officer, in taking the decisions required by subsection (1)(a) and (b) above (except (a)(i) and (vi) and (b)(ii)), shall have regard to the same considerations as those which a court is required to have regard to in taking the corresponding decisions under paragraph [2(1)][4] of Part I of Schedule 1 to the Bail Act 1976 [(disregarding paragraph 2(2) of that Part)].[5]]

(6A) In this section—

"local authority accommodation" means accommodation provided by or on behalf of a local authority (within the meaning of the Children Act 1989);
["minimum age" means the age specified in [section 63B(3)(b) below][6]];[7]
"secure accommodation" means accommodation provided for the purpose of restricting liberty;
["sexual offence" means an offence specified in Part 2 of Schedule 15 to the Criminal Justice Act 2003;
"violent offence" means murder or an offence specified in Part 1 of that Schedule];[8]

and any reference, in relation to an arrested juvenile charged with a violent or sexual offence, to protecting the public from serious harm from him shall be construed as a reference to protecting members of the public from death or serious personal injury, whether physical or psychological, occasioned by further such offences committed by him.

NOTES

[1] Subsection substituted by Criminal Justice Act 2003 (c.44), s.5(1), (2)(a)(i); amendment in force August 1, 2004 (in relation to Cleveland, Greater Manchester, Humberside, Merseyside, metropolitan police district, Nottinghamshire and West Yorkshire police areas), and on a date to be appointed in relation to other purposes.

[2] Subsection further substituted by Drugs Act 2005 (c.17), s.23(1), Sch.1, paras 1, 3(a); amendment in force on a date to be appointed.

[3] Words inserted by Criminal Justice Act 2003 (c.44), s.5(1), (2)(a)(ii); amendment in force August 1, 2004 (in relation to Cleveland, Greater Manchester, Humberside, Merseyside, metropolitan police district, Nottinghamshire and West Yorkshire police areas), and on a date to be appointed in relation to other purposes.

[4] Words substituted by Criminal Justice Act 2003 (c.44), s.331, Sch.36, Pt 1, para.5(b); amendment in force April 5, 2004.

[5] Words inserted by Criminal Justice Act 2003 (c.44), s.331, Sch.36, Pt 1, para.5(b); amendment in force April 5 2004.

[6] Words substituted by Drugs Act 2005 (c.17), s.23(1), Sch.1, paras 1, 3(b); amendment in force on a date to be appointed.

[7] Definition inserted by Criminal Justice Act 2003 (c.44), s.5(1), (2)(b); amendment in force 1 August 2004 (in relation to Cleveland, Greater Manchester, Humberside, Merseyside, metropolitan police district, Nottinghamshire and West Yorkshire police areas), and on a date to be appointed in relation to other purposes.

[8] Definitions substituted by Criminal Justice Act 2003 (c.44), s.304, Sch.32, Pt 1, para.44; amendment in force on a date to be appointed.

s 39 Responsibilities in relation to persons detained

(6)   Where—   App–039

(a)   an officer of higher rank than the custody officer [(or, if the custody officer is a staff custody officer, any police officer or any police employee)] gives directions relating to a person in police detention;[1] and

(b)   the directions are at variance—

(i)   with any decision made or action taken by the custody officer in the performance of a duty imposed on him under this Part of this Act; or

(ii)   with any decision or action which would but for the directions have been made or taken by him in the performance of such a duty,

the custody officer shall refer the matter at once to an officer of the rank of superintendent or above who is responsible for the police station for which the custody officer is acting as custody officer.

[(7)   In subsection (6) above—

"police employee" means a person employed under section 15 of the Police Act 1996;

"staff custody officer" has the same meaning as in the Police Reform Act 2002.][2]

NOTES

[1] Words inserted by Serious Organised Crime and Police Act 2005 (c.15), s.121(7)(a); amendment in force on a date to be appointed.

[2] Subsection inserted by Serious Organised Crime and Police Act 2005 (c.15), s.121(7)(b); amendment in force on a date to be appointed.

s 40 Review of police detention

(9)   Where a person has been kept in police detention by virtue of section 37(9) [or 37D(5)][1] above, section 37(1) to (6) shall not have effect in relation to him but it shall be the duty of the review officer to determine whether he is yet in a fit state.   App–040

NOTE

[1] Words inserted by Criminal Justice Act 2003 (c.44), s.28, Sch.2, paras 1, 4; amendment in force January 29, 2004.

s 40A Use of telephone for review under s 40

[(1)   A review under section 40(1)(b) may be carried out by means of a discussion, conducted by telephone, with one or more persons at the police station where the arrested person is held.   App–040A

(2)   But subsection (1) does not apply if—

(a) the review is of a kind authorised by regulations under section 45A to be carried out using video-conferencing facilities; and

(b) it is reasonably practicable to carry it out in accordance with those regulations.][1]

NOTE

[1] Words substituted by Criminal Justice Act 2003 (c.44), s.6; amendment in force January 20, 2004.

s 41 Limits on period of detention without charge

App–042

(2) The time from which the period of detention of a person is to be calculated (in this Act referred to as "the relevant time")—

(a) in the case of a person to whom this paragraph applies, shall be—

(i) the time at which that person arrives at the relevant police station; or
(ii) the time 24 hours after the time of that person's arrest,

whichever is the earlier;

(b) in the case of a person arrested outside England and Wales, shall be—

(i) the time at which that person arrives at the first police station to which he is taken in the police areas in England and Wales in which the offence for which he was arrested is being investigated or
(ii) the time 24 hours after the time of that person's entry into England and Wales,

whichever is the earlier;

(c) in the case of a person who—

(i) attends voluntarily at a police station; or
(ii) accompanies a constable to a police station without having been arrested,

and is arrested at the police station, the time of his arrest;

[(ca) in the case of a person who attends a police station to answer to bail granted under section 30A, the time when he arrives at the police station;][1]

(d) in any other case, except where subsection (5) below applies, shall be the time at which the person arrested arrives at the first police station to which he is taken after his arrest.

NOTE

[1] Words inserted by Criminal Justice Act 2003 (c.44), s.12, Sch.1, paras 1, 8; amendment in force January 20, 2004.

s 42 Authorisation of continued detention

App–043

(1) Where a police officer of the rank of superintendent or above who is responsible for the police station at which a person is detained has reasonable grounds for believing that—

(a)   the detention of that person without charge is necessary to secure or preserve evidence relating to an offence for which he is under arrest or to obtain such evidence by questioning him;

[(b) an offence for which he is under arrest is an [indictable][1] offence; and][2]

(c)   the investigation is being conducted diligently and expeditiously;

he may authorise the keeping of that person in police detention for a period expiring at or before 36 hours after the relevant time.

NOTES

[1] Word substituted by Serious Organised Crime and Police Act 2005 (c.15), s.111, Sch.7, Pt 3, para.43(1), (7); amendment in force on a date to be appointed.

[2] Subsection substituted by Criminal Justice Act 2003 (c.44), s.7; amendment in force January 20, 2004.

s 43 Warrants of further detention

(4)   A person's further detention is only justified for the purposes of this section or   **App–044**
section 44 below if—

(a)   his detention without charge is necessary to secure or preserve evidence relating to an offence for which he is under arrest or to obtain such evidence by questioning him;

(b)   an offence for which he is under arrest is [an indictable offence];[1] and

(c)   the investigation is being conducted diligently and expeditiously.

NOTE

[1] Words substituted by Serious Organised Crime and Police Act 2005 (c.15), s.111, Sch.7, Pt 3, para.43(1), (8); amendment in force on a date to be appointed.

s 45A Use of video-conferencing facilities for decisions about detention

(2)   Those functions are—   **App–047**

(a)   the functions in relation to an arrested person taken to[, or answering to bail at,][1] a police station that is not a designated police station which, in the case of an arrested person taken to a station that is a designated police station, are functions of a custody officer under section 37, 38 or 40 above; and

(b)   the function of carrying out a review under section 40(1)(b) above (review, by an officer of at least the rank of inspector, of the detention of person arrested but not charged).

NOTE

[1] Words inserted by Criminal Justice Act 2003 (c.44), s.12, Sch.1, paras 1, 9; amendment in force January 20, 2004.

Detention—Miscellaneous

s 46 Detention after charge

App–048

(2) If he is to be brought before a magistrates' court [in the local justice][1] area in which the police station at which he was charged is situated, he shall be brought before such a court as soon as is practicable and in any event not later than the first sitting after he is charged with the offence.

(3) If no magistrates' court [in that area] is due to sit either on the day on which he is charged or on the next day, the custody officer for the police station at which he was charged shall inform the [designated officer] for the area that there is a person in the area to whom subsection (2) above applies.[2]

(4) If the person charged is to be brought before a magistrates' court [in a local justice] area other than that in which the police station at which he was charged is situated, he shall be removed to that area as soon as is practicable and brought before such a court as soon as is practicable after his arrival in the area and in any event not later than the first sitting of a magistrates' court [in that area] after his arrival in the area.[3]

(5) If no magistrates' court [in that area] is due to sit either on the day on which he arrives in the area or on the next day—

  (a) he shall be taken to a police station in the area; and

  (b) the custody officer at that station shall inform [the designated officer] in that area that there is a person in the area to whom subsection (4) applies.[4]

(6) Subject to subsection (8) below, where [the designated officer for a local justice] area has been informed—

  (a) under subsection (3) above that there is a person in the area to whom subsection (2) above applies; or

  (b) under subsection (5) above that there is a person in the area to whom subsection (4) above applies,

[the designated officer] shall arrange for a magistrates' court to sit not later than the day next following the relevant day.[5]

(7) In this section "the relevant day"—

  (a) in relation to a person who is to be brought before a magistrates' court [in the local justice] area in which the police station at which he was charged is situated, means the day on which he was charged; and

  (b) in relation to a person who is to be brought before a magistrates' court [in any other local justice] area, means the day on which he arrives in the area.[6]

(8) Where the day next following the relevant day is Christmas Day, Good Friday or a Sunday, the duty of the [designated officer][7] under subsection (6) above is a duty to arrange for a magistrates' court to sit not later than the first day after the relevant day which is not one of those days.

NOTES

[1 to 7] Words in square brackets substituted by Courts Act 2003 (c.39), s.109(1), Sch.8, para.282 (1) to (8); amendments in force April 1, 2005.

s 46A Power of arrest for failure to answer to police bail

[(1A) A person who has been released on bail under section 37(7)(a) or 37C(2)(b)   **App–049**
above may be arrested without warrant by a constable if the constable has
reasonable grounds for suspecting that the person has broken any of the
conditions of bail.]¹

NOTE

¹ Subsection inserted by Criminal Justice Act 2003 (c.44), s.28, Sch.2, paras 1, 5; amendment in
force January 29, 2004.

s 47 Bail after arrest

(1) [Subject to the following provisions of this section]¹, a release on bail of a per-   **App–050**
son under this Part of this Act shall be a release on bail granted in accordance
with [sections 3, 3A, 5 and 5A of the Bail Act 1976 as they apply to bail granted
by a constable].

[(1A) The normal powers to impose conditions of bail shall be available to him where
a custody officer releases a person on bail under section [37(7)(a) above or sec-
tion]² 38(1) above (including that subsection as applied by section 40(10) above)
but not in any other cases. In this subsection, "the normal powers to impose
conditions of bail" has the meaning given in section 3(6) of the Bail Act 1976.]

[(1B) No application may be made under section 5B of the Bail Act 1976 if a person
is released on bail under section 37(7) or 37(2)(b) above.

(1C) Subsections (1D) to (1F) below apply where a person released on bail under
section 37(7)(a) or 37C(2)(b) above is on bail subject to conditions.

(1D) The person shall not be entitled to make an application under section 43B of
the Magistrates' Courts Act 1980.

(1E) A magistrates' court may, on an application by or on behalf of the person, vary
the conditions of bail; and in this subsection "vary" has the same meaning as
in the Bail Act 1976.

(1F) Where a magistrates' court varies the conditions of bail under subsection (1E)
above, that bail shall not lapse but shall continue subject to the conditions as so
varied.]³

[(3A) Where a custody officer grants bail to a person subject to a duty to appear
before a magistrates' court, he shall appoint for the appearance—

(a) a date which is not later than the first sitting of the court after the person is
charged with the offence; or

(b) where he is informed by the [designated officer for the relevant local justice]⁴
area that the appearance cannot be accommodated until a later date, that later
date.]

(6) Where a person [who has been granted bail [under this Part]⁵ and either has
attended at the police station in accordance with the grant of bail or has been
arrested under section 46A above is detained at a police station], any time during which he was in police detention prior to being granted bail shall be
included as part of any period which falls to be calculated under this Part of
this Act.

(7)   Where a person who was released on bail [under this Part][6] subject to a duty to attend at a police station is re-arrested, the provisions of this Part of this Act shall apply to him as they apply to a person arrested for the first time[; but this subsection does not apply to a person who is arrested under section 46A above or has attended a police station in accordance with the grant of bail (and who accordingly is deemed by section 34(7) above to have been arrested for an offence)].

NOTES

[1] Words substituted by Criminal Justice Act 2003 (c.44), s.28, Sch.2, paras 1, 6(1), (2); amendment in force January 29, 2004.

[2] Words inserted by Criminal Justice Act 2003 (c.44), s.28, Sch.2, paras 1, 6(1), (3); amendment in force January 29, 2004.

[3] Subsections inserted by Criminal Justice Act 2003 (c.44), s.28, Sch.2, paras 1, 6(1), (4); amendment in force January 29, 2004.

[4] Words substituted by Courts Act 2003 (c.39), s.109(1), Sch.8, para.283; amendment in force April 1, 2005.

[5] Words inserted by Criminal Justice Act 2003 (c.44), s.12, Sch.1, paras 1, 10(a); amendment in force January 20, 2004.

[6] Words inserted by Criminal Justice Act 2003 (c.44), s.12, Sch.1, paras 1, 10(b); amendment in force January 20, 2004.

s 47A Early administrative hearings conducted by justices' clerks

App–051   Where a person has been charged with an offence at a police station, any requirement imposed under this Part for the person to appear or be brought before a magistrates' court shall be taken to be satisfied if the person appears or is brought before [a justices' clerk][1] in order for the clerk to conduct a hearing under section 50 of the Crime and Disorder Act 1998 (early administrative hearings).

NOTE

[1] Words substituted by Courts Act 2003 (c.39), s.109(1), Sch.8, para.284; amendment in force April 1, 2005.

Part V

Questioning and Treatment of Persons by Police

. . .

s 54 Searches of detained persons

App–057   (1)   The custody officer at a police station shall ascertain [. . .][1] everything which a person has with him when he is—

(a)   brought to the station after being arrested elsewhere or after being committed to custody by an order or sentence of a court; or

[(b) arrested at the station or detained there[, as a person falling within section 34(7), under section 37 above].]

[(2) The custody officer may record or cause to be recorded all or any of the things which he ascertains under subsection (1).

(2A) In the case of an arrested person, any such record may be made as part of his custody record.]²

NOTES

¹ Words repealed by Criminal Justice Act 2003 (c.44), ss.8(1), 332, Sch.37, Pt 1; amendment in force January 20, 2004.
² Subsections substituted by Criminal Justice Act 2003 (c.44), s.8(2); amendment in force January 20, 2004.

s 54A Searches and examination to ascertain identity

[(13) Nothing in this section applies to a person arrested under an extradition arrest power.]¹   **App–058**

NOTE

¹ Subsection inserted by Extradition Act 2003 (c.41), s.169(1), (2); amendment in force January 1, 2004.

s 55 Intimate searches

[(3A) A drug offence search shall not be carried out unless the appropriate consent has been given in writing.   **App–059**

(3B) Where it is proposed that a drug offence search be carried out, an appropriate officer shall inform the person who is to be subject to it—

(a)   of the giving of the authorisation for it; and
(b)   of the grounds for giving the authorisation.]¹

[(10A)If the intimate search is a drug offence search, the custody record relating to that person shall also state—

(a)   the authorisation by virtue of which the search was carried out;
(b)   the grounds for giving the authorisation; and
(c)   the fact that the appropriate consent was given.]²

(11) The information required to be recorded by [subsections (10) and (10A)]³ above shall be recorded as soon as practicable after the completion of the search.

[(13A)Where the appropriate consent to a drug offence search of any person was refused without good cause, in any proceedings against that person for an offence—

(a)   the court, determining where there is a case to answer;
(b)   a judge, in deciding whether to grant an application made by the accused

under paragraph 2 of Schedule 3 to the Crime and Disorder Act 1998 (applications for dismissal); and

(c) the court or jury, in determining whether that person is guilty of the offence charged,

may draw such inferences from the refusal as appeal proper.][4]

[(14A). . .][5]

(17) In this section—

"the appropriate criminal intent" means an intent to commit an offence under—

(a) section 5(3) of the Misuse of Drugs Act 1971 (possession of controlled drug with intent to supply to another); or

(b) section 68(2) of the Customs and Excise Management Act 1979 (exportation etc with intent to evade a prohibition or restriction);

["appropriate officer" means—

(a) a constable;

(b) a person who is designated as a detention officer in pursuance of section 38 of the Police Reform Act 2002 if his designation applies paragraph 33D of Schedule 4 to that Act, or

(c) a person who is designated as a staff custody officer in pursuance of section 38 of that Act if his designation applies paragraph 35C of Schedule 4 to that Act;][6]

"Class A drug" has the meaning assigned to it by section 2(1)(b) of the Misuse of Drugs Act 1971;

"drug offence search" means an intimate search for a Class A drug which an officer has authorised by virtue of subsection (1)(b) above; and

"suitably qualified person" means—

(a) a registered medical practitioner; or

(b) a registered nurse.

NOTES

[1] Subsections inserted by the Drugs Act 2005 (c.17), s.3(1), (2); amendment in force on a date to be appointed.
[2] Subsection inserted by Drugs Act 2005 (c.17), s.3(1), (3); amendment in force on a date to be appointed.
[3] Words substituted by Drugs Act 2005 (c.17), s.3(1), (4); amendment in force on a date to be appointed.
[4] Subsection inserted by Drugs Act 2005 (c.17) s.3(1), (5); amendment in force on a date to be appointed.
[5] Repealed by Serious Organised Crime and Police Act 2005 (c.15), ss.59, 174(2), Sch.4, paras 43, 45, Sch.17, Pt 2; amendment in force on a date to be appointed.
[6] Definition inserted by Drugs Act 2005 (c.17), s.3(1), (6); amendment in force on a date to be appointed.

[s 55A X-rays and ultrasound scans

App–059A (1) If an officer of at least the rank of inspector has reasonable grounds for believing that a person who has been arrested for an offence and is in police detention—

(a) may have swallowed a Class A drug, and

(b) was in possession of it with the appropriate criminal intent before his arrest,

the officer may authorise that an x-ray is taken of the person or an ultrasound scan is carried out on the person (or both).

(2) An x-ray must not be taken of a person and an ultrasound scan must not be carried out on him unless the appropriate consent has been given in writing.

(3) If it is proposed that an x-ray is taken or an ultrasound scan is carried out, an appropriate officer must inform the person who is to be subject to it—

(a) of the giving of the authorisation for it, and

(b) of the grounds for giving the authorisation.

(4) An x-ray may be taken or an ultrasound scan carried out only by a suitably qualified person and only at—

(a) a hospital,

(b) a registered medical practitioner's surgery, or

(c) some other place used for medical purposes.

(5) The custody record of the person must also state—

(a) the authorisation by virtue of which the x-ray was taken or the ultrasound scan was carried out,

(b) the grounds for giving the authorisation, and

(c) the fact that the appropriate consent was given.

(6) The information required to be recorded by subsection (5) must be recorded as soon as practicable after the x-ray has been taken or ultrasound scan carried out (as the case may be).

(7) Every annual report—

(a) under section 22 of the Police Act 1996, or

(b) made by the Commissioner of Police of the Metropolis,

must contain information about x-rays which have been taken and ultrasound scans which have been carried out under this section in the area to which the report relates during the period to which it relates.

(8) The information about such x-rays and ultrasound scans must be presented separately and must include—

(a) the total number of x-rays;

(b) the total number of ultrasound scans;

(c) the results of the x-rays;

(d) the results of the ultrasound scans.

(9) If the appropriate consent to an x-ray or ultrasound scan of any person is refused without good cause, in any proceedings against that person for an offence—

(a) the court, in determining whether there is a case to answer,

(b) a judge, in deciding whether to grant an application made by the accused under paragraph 2 of Schedule 3 to the Crime and Disorder Act 1998 (applications for dismissal), and

(c) the court or jury, in determining whether that person is guilty of the offence charged,

may draw such inferences from the refusal as appear proper.

(10) In this section "the appropriate criminal intent", "appropriate officer", "Class A drug" and "suitably qualified person" have the same meanings as in section 55 above."][1]

NOTE

[1] Section inserted by Drugs Act 2005 (c.17), s.5(1); amendment in force on a date to be appointed.

s 56 Right to have someone informed when arrested

App–060   (2) Delay is only permitted—

(a) in the case of a person who is in police detention for [an indictable offence];[1] and
(b) if an officer of at least the rank of [inspector] authorises it.

(5) [Subject to subsection (5A)] below an officer may only authorise delay where he has reasonable grounds for believing that telling the named person of the arrest—

(a) will lead to interference with or harm to evidence connected with [an indictable offence][2] or interference with or physical injury to other persons; or
(b) will lead to the alerting of other persons suspected of having committed such an offence but not yet arrested for it; or
(c) will hinder the recovery of any property obtained as a result of such an offence.

[(5A) An officer may also authorise delay where he has reasonable grounds for believing that—

(a) the person detained for [the indictable offence][3] has benefited from his criminal conduct, and
(b) the recovery of the value of the property constituting the benefit will be hindered by telling the named person of the arrest.]

NOTES

[1] Words substituted by Serious Organised Crime and Police Act 2005 (c.15), s.111, Sch.7, Pt 3, para.43(1), (9)(a); amendment in force on a date to be appointed.
[2] Words substituted by Serious Organised Crime and Police Act 2005 (c.15), s.111, Sch.7, Pt 3, para.43(1), (9)(a); amendment in force on a date to be appointed.
[3] Words substituted by Serious Organised Crime and Police Act 2005 (c.15), s.111, Sch.7, Pt 3, para.43(1), (9)(b); amendment in force on a date to be appointed.

s 58 Access to legal advice

App–062   (6) Delay in compliance with a request is only permitted—

(a) in the case of a person who is in police detention for [an indictable offence];[1] and
(b) if an officer of at least the rank of superintendent authorises it.

(8) [Subject to subsection (8A)] below an officer may only authorise delay where he has reasonable grounds for believing that the exercise of the right conferred by

subsection (1) above at the time when the person detained desires to exercise it—

(a) will lead to interference with or harm to evidence connected with [an indictable offence] or interference with or physical injury to other persons;[2] or

(b) will lead to the alerting of other persons suspected of having committed such an offence but not yet arrested for it; or

(c) will hinder the recovery of any property obtained as a result of such an offence.

[(8A) An officer may also authorise delay where he has reasonable grounds for believing that—

(a) the person detained for [the indictable offence][3] has benefited from his criminal conduct, and

(b) the recovery of the value of the property constituting the benefit will be hindered by the exercise of the right conferred by subsection (1) above.

NOTES

[1] Words substituted by Serious Organised Crime and Police Act 2005 (c.15), s.111, Sch.7, Pt 3, para.43(1), (10)(a); amendment in force on a date to be appointed.
[2] Words substituted by Serious Organised Crime and Police Act 2005 (c.15), s.111, Sch.7, Pt 3, para.43(1), (10)(a); amendment in force on a date to be appointed.
[3] Words substituted by Serious Organised Crime and Police Act 2005 (c.15), s.111, Sch.7, Pt 3, para.43(1), (10)(b); amendment in force on a date to be appointed.

s 61 Finger-printing

[(3) The fingerprints of a person detained at a police station may be taken without the appropriate consent if—   App–065

(a) he is detained in consequence of his arrest for a recordable offence; and

(b) he has not had his fingerprints taken in the course of the investigation of the offence by the police.][1]

[(3A) [Where a person mentioned in paragraph (a) of subsection (3) or (4) has already had his fingerprints taken in the course of the investigation of the offence by the police],[2] that fact shall be disregarded for the purposes of that subsection if—

(a) the fingerprints taken on the previous occasion do not constitute a complete set of his fingerprints; or

(b) some or all of the fingerprints taken on the previous occasion are not of sufficient quality to allow satisfactory analysis, comparison or matching (whether in the case in question or generally).]

[(4) The fingerprints of a person detained at a police station may be taken without the appropriate consent if—

(a) he has been charged with a recordable offence or informed that he will be reported for such an offence; and

(b) he has not had his fingerprints taken in the course of the investigation of the offence by the police.][3]

(5) An officer may give an authorisation under [subsection (4A)][4] above orally or

in writing but, if he gives it orally, he shall confirm it in writing as soon as is practicable.

[(6A) A constable may take a person's fingerprints without the appropriate consent if—

    (a) the constable reasonably suspects that the person is committing or attempting to commit an offence, or has committed or attempted to commit an offence; and

    (b) either of the two conditions mentioned in subsection (6B) is met.

(6B) The conditions are that—

    (a) the name of the person is unknown to, and cannot be readily ascertained by, the constable;

    (b) the constable has reasonable grounds for doubting whether a name furnished by the person as his name is his real name.

(6C) The taking of fingerprints by virtue of subsection (6A) does not count for any of the purposes of this Act as taking them in the course of the investigation of an offence by the police.][5]

(7) In a case where by virtue of [subsection (3), (4),][6] [(6) or (6A)][7] above a person's fingerprints are taken without the appropriate consent—

    (a) he shall be told the reason before his fingerprints are taken; and

    (b) the reason shall be recorded as soon as is practicable after the fingerprints are taken.

[(7A) If a person's fingerprints are taken at a police station [or by virtue of subsection (6A) at a place other than a police station][8], whether with or without the appropriate consent—

    (a) before the fingerprints are taken, an officer [or, in a subsection (6A) case, the constable][9] shall inform him that they may be the subject of a speculative search; and

    (b) the fact that the person has been informed of this possibility shall be recorded as soon as is practicable after the fingerprints have been taken.]

[(8A) Where a person's fingerprints are taken electronically, they must be taken only in such manner, and using such devices, as the Secretary of State has approved for the purposes of electronic fingerprinting.][10]

(9) Nothing in this section—

    (a) affects any power conferred by paragraph 18(2) of Schedule 2 to the Immigration Act 1971[, section 141 of the Immigration and Asylum Act 1999 or regulations made under section 144 of that Act][11]; or

    (b) [applies to a person arrested or detained under the terrorism provisions.]

[(10) Nothing in this section applies to a person arrested under an extradition arrest power.][12]

NOTES

[1] Words substituted by Criminal Justice Act 2003 (c.44), s.9(1), (2); amendment in force April 5, 2004.

[2] Words substituted by Criminal Justice Act 2003 (c.44), s.9(1), (3); amendment in force April 5, 2004.

³ Subsection substituted by Criminal Justice Act 2003 (c.44), s.9(1), (2); amendment in force April 5, 2004.
⁴ Words substituted by Criminal Justice Act 2003 (c.44), s.9(1), (4); amendment in force April 5, 2004.
⁵ Subsections inserted by Serious Organised Crime and Police Act 2005 (c.15), s.117(1), (2); amendment in force on a date to be appointed.
⁶ Words substituted by Criminal Justice Act 2003 (c.44), s.9(1), (5); amendment in force April 5, 2004.
⁷ Words substituted by Serious Organised Crime and Police Act 2005 (c.15), s.117(1), (3); amendment in force on a date to be appointed.
⁸ Words inserted by Serious Organised Crime and Police Act 2005 (c.15), s.117(1), (4)(a); amendment in force on a date to be appointed.
⁹ Words inserted by Serious Organised Crime and Police Act 2005 (c.15), s.117(1), (4)(b); amendment in force on a date to be appointed.
¹⁰ Words inserted by Criminal Justice and Police Act 2001 (c.16), s.78(7); amendment in force on a date to be appointed.
¹¹ Words inserted by Immigration and Asylum Act 1999 (c.33), s.169(1), Sch.14, para.80(1), (4); amendment in force on a date to be appointed.
¹² Subsection inserted by Extradition Act 2003 (c.41), s.169(1), (3); amendment in force January 1, 2004.

[s 61A Impressions of footwear

(1) Except as provided by this section, no impression of a person's footwear may be taken without the appropriate consent.   App–065A

(2) Consent to the taking of an impression of a person's footwear must be in writing if it is given at a time when he is at a police station.

(3) Where a person is detained at a police station, an impression of his footwear may be taken without the appropriate consent if—

   (a) he is detained in consequence of his arrest for a recordable offence, or has been charged with a recordable offence, or informed that he will be reported for a recordable offence; and

   (b) he has not had an impression taken of his footwear in the course of the investigation of the offence by the police.

(4) Where a person mentioned in paragraph (a) of subsection (3) above has already has an impression taken of his footwear in the course of the investigation of the offence by the police, that fact shall be disregarded for the purposes of that subsection if the impression of his footwear taken previously is—

   (a) incomplete; or
   (b) is not of sufficient quality to allow satisfactory analysis, comparison or matching (whether in the case in question of generally).

(5) If an impression of a person's footwear is taken at a police station, whether with or without the appropriate consent—

   (a) before it is taken, an officer shall inform him that is may be the subject of a speculative search; and

   (b) the fact that the person has been informed of this possibility shall be recorded as soon as is practicable after the impression has been taken, and if he is detained at a police station, the record shall be made on his custody record.

(6) In a case where, by virtue of subsection (3) above, an impression of a person's footwear is taken without the appropriate consent—

(a) he shall be told the reason before it is taken; and
(b) the reason shall be recorded on his custody record as soon as is practicable after the impression is taken.

(7) The power to take an impression of the footwear of a person detained at a police station without the appropriate consent shall be exercisable by an constable.

(8) Nothing in this section applies to any person—

(a) arrested or detained under the terrorism provisions;
(b) arrested under an extradition arrest power.]¹

NOTE

¹ Section inserted by Serious Organised Crime and Police Act 2005 (c.15), s.118(1), (2); amendment in force on a date to be appointed.

s 62 Intimate samples

App–066

(10) Where the appropriate consent to the taking of an intimate sample from a person was refused without good cause, in any proceedings against that person for an offence—

(a) the court, in determining—

(i) [whether to commit that person for trial]¹; or
(ii) whether there is a case to answer; and

[(aa) a judge, in deciding whether to grant an application made by the accused under paragraph 2 of Schedule 3 to the Crime and Disorder Act 1998 (applications for dismissal); and]²
(b) the court or jury, in determining whether that person is guilty of the offence charged,

may draw such inferences from the refusal as appear proper.

NOTES

¹ Words repealed by the Criminal Justice Act 2003 (c.44), ss.41, 332, Sch.3, Pt 2, para.56(1), (2)(a), Sch.37, Pt 4; amendment in force on a date to be appointed.
² Words substituted for s.62(10)(aa)(i)–(ii) by Criminal Justice Act 2003 (c.44), s.41, Sch.3, Pt 2, para.56(1), (2)(b); amendment in force on a date to be appointed.

s 63 Other samples

App–067

[(2A) A non-intimate sample may be taken from a person without the appropriate consent if two conditions are satisfied.

(2B) The first is that the person is in police detention in consequence of his arrest for a recordable offence.

(2C) The second is that—

(a) he has not had a non-intimate sample of the same type and from the same part of the body taken in the course of the investigation of the offence by the police, or

(b)   he has had such a sample taken but it proved insufficient.]¹

(3)   A non-intimate sample may be taken from a person without the appropriate consent if—

(a)   he [. . .]² is being held in custody by the police on the authority of a court; and
(b)   an officer of at least the rank of [inspector] authorises it to be taken without the appropriate consent.

[(3A) A non-intimate sample may be taken from a person (whether or not he [is in police detention or held in custody by the police on the authority of a court]³) without the appropriate consent if—

(a)   he has been charged with a recordable offence or informed that he will be reported for such an offence; and
(b)   either he has not had a non-intimate sample taken from him in the course of the investigation of the offence by the police or he had a non-intimate sample taken from him but either it was not suitable for the same means of analysis or, though so suitable, the sample proved insufficient.

[(8A) In a case where by virtue of subsection [(2A), (3A)]⁴ [, (3B) or (3C) above] a sample is taken from a person without the appropriate consent—

(a)   he shall be told the reason before the sample is taken; and
(b)   the reason shall be recorded as soon as practicable after the sample is taken.]

[(9A) Where a non-intimate sample consisting of a skin impression is taken electronically from a person, it must be taken only in such a manner, and using such devices, as the Secretary of State has approved for the purpose of the electronic taking of such an impression.]⁵

[(11) Nothing in this section applies to a person arrested under an extradition arrest power.]⁶

Notes

¹ Subsections inserted by Criminal Justice Act 2003 (c.44), s.10(1), (2); amendment in force April 5, 2004.
² Words repealed by Criminal Justice Act 2003 (c.44), ss.10(1), (3), 332, Sch.37, Pt 1; amendment in force April 5, 2004.
³ Words substituted by Criminal Justice Act 2003 (c.44), s.10(1), (4); amendment in force April 5, 2004.
⁴ Words substituted by Criminal Justice Act 2003 (c.44), s.10(1), (5); amendment in force April 5, 2004.
⁵ Subsection inserted by Criminal Justice and Police Act 2001 (c.16), s.80(4); amendment in force on a date to be appointed.
⁶ Subsection inserted by Extradition Act 2003 (c.41), s.169(1), (4); amendment in force January 1, 2004.

s 63A Fingerprints and samples: supplementary provisions

[(1) Where a person has been arrested on suspicion of being involved in a recordable offence or has been charged with such an offence or has been informed that he will be reported for such an offence, fingerprints[, impressions of footwear]¹ samples or the information derived from samples taken under any power conferred by this Part of this Act from the person may be checked against—   **App–068**

147

(a) other fingerprints[, impressions of footwear]^2 or samples to which the person seeking to check has access and which are held by or on behalf of [any one or more relevant law-enforcement authorities or which] are held in connection with or as a result of an investigation of an offence;

(b) information derived from other samples if the information is contained in records to which the person seeking to check has access and which are held as mentioned in paragraph (a) above.]

[(1ZA) Fingerprints taken by virtue of section 61(6A) above may be checked against other fingerprints to which the person seeking to check has access and which are held by or on behalf of any one or more relevant law-enforcement authorities or which are held in connection with or as a result of an investigation of an offence.]^3

[(1A) In subsection (1) [and (1ZA)]^4 above "relevant law-enforcement authority" means—

(a) a police force;

(b) [the Serious Organised Crime Agency;]^5

(d) a public authority (not falling within paragraphs (a) to (c)) with functions in any part of the British Islands which consist of or include the investigation of crimes or the charging of offenders;

(e) any person with functions in any country or territory outside the United Kingdom which—

(i) correspond to those of a police force; or

(ii) otherwise consist of or include the investigation of conduct contrary to the law of that country or territory, or the apprehension of persons guilty of such conduct;

(f) any person with functions under any international agreement which consist of or include the investigation of conduct which is—

(i) unlawful under the law of one or more places,

(ii) prohibited by such an agreement, or

(iii) contrary to international law,

or the apprehension of persons guilty of such conduct.

(1C) Where—

(a) fingerprints[, impressions of footwear]^6 or samples have been taken from any person in connection with the investigation of an offence but otherwise than in circumstances to which subsection (1) above applies, and

(b) that person has given his consent in writing to the use in a speculative search of the fingerprints[, of the impressions of footwear]^7 or of the samples and of information derived from them,

the fingerprints [or impressions of footwear]^8 or, as the case may be, those samples and that information may be checked against any of the fingerprints[, impressions of footwear],^{9} samples or information mentioned in paragraph (a) or (b) of that subsection.

NOTES

$^{1\ and\ 2}$ Words inserted by Serious Organised Crime and Police Act 2005 (c.15), s.118(1), (3)(a); amendment in force on a date to be appointed.

3   Subsection inserted by Serious Organised Crime and Police Act 2005 (c.15), s.117(5)(a); amendment in force on a date to be appointed.
4   Words inserted by Serious Organised Crime and Police Act 2005 (c.15), s.117(5)(b); amendment in force on a date to be appointed.
5   Words substituted by Serious Organised Crime and Police Act 2005 (c.15), s.59, Sch.4, Paras 43, 46; amendment in force on a date to be appointed.
6 to 9   Words inserted by Serious Organised Crime and Police Act 2005 (c.15), s.118(1), (3)(b); amendments in force on a date to be appointed.

[s 63B Testing for presence of Class A drugs

(1)   A sample of urine or a non-intimate sample may be taken form a person in police detention for the purpose of ascertaining whether he has any specified Class A drug in his body if [—   **App–069**

   (a)   either the arrest condition or the charge condition is met;
   (b)   both the age condition and the request condition are met; and
   (c)   the notification condition is met in relation to the arrest condition, the charge condition or the age condition (as the case may be)].[1]

[(1A) The arrest condition is that the person concerned has been arrested for an offence but has not been charged with that offence and either—

   (a)   the offence is a trigger offence; or
   (b)   a police officer of at least the rank of inspector has reasonable grounds for suspecting that the misuse by that person of a specific Class A drug caused or contributed to the offence and has authorised the sample to be taken.][2]

(2)   [The charge condition is either][3]—

   (a)   that the person concerned has been charged with a trigger offence; or
   (b)   that the person concerned has been charged with an offence and a police officer of at least the rank of inspector, who has reasonable grounds for suspecting that the misuse by that person of any specified Class A drug caused or contributed to the offence, has authorised the sample to be taken.

[(3)   The second condition is that the person concerned has attained the age of [14].[4]]

[(3)   The age condition is—

   (a)   if the arrest condition is met, that the person concerned has attained the age of 18;
   (b)   if the charge condition is met, that he was attained the age of 14.][5]

(4)   The [request][6] condition is that a police officer has requested the person concerned to give the sample.

[(4A) The notification condition is that—

   (a)   the relevant chief officer has been notified by the Secretary of State that appropriate arrangements have been made for the police area as a whole, or for the particular police station, in which the person is in police detention, and
   (b)   the notice has not been withdrawn.

(4B) For the purposes of subsection (4A) above, appropriate arrangements are arrangements for the taking of samples under this section from whichever of the following is specified in the notification—

   (a)   persons in respect of whom the arrest condition is met;

(b) persons in respect of whom the charge condition is met;

(c) persons who have not attained the age of 18.][7]

(5) Before requesting the person concerned to give a sample, an officer must—

(a) warn him if, when so requested, he fails without good cause to do so he may be liable to prosecution, and

(b) in a case within subsection [(1A)(b) or][8] (2)(b) above, inform him of the giving of the authorisation and of the grounds in question.

[(5A) In the case of a person who has not attained the age of 17—

(a) the making of the request under subsection (4) above;

(b) the giving of the warning and (where applicable) the information under subsection (5) above; and

(c) the taking of the sample, may not take place except in the presence of an appropriate adult.][9]

[(5B) If a sample if taken under this section from a person in respect of whom the arrest condition is met no other sample may be taken from him under this section during the same continuous period of detention but—

(a) if the charge condition is also met in respect of him at any time during that period, the sample must be treated as a sample taken by virtue of the fact that the charge condition is met;

(b) the fact that the sample if to be so treated must be recorded in the person's custody record.

(5C) Despite subsection (1)(a) above, a sample may be taken from a person under this section if—

(a) he was arrested for an offence (the first offence),

(b) the arrest condition is met but the charge condition if not met,

(c) before a sample is taken by virtue of subsection (1) above he would (but for his arrest as mentioned in paragraph (d) before) be required to be released from police detention,

(d) he continues to be in police detention by virtue of his having been arrested for an offence not falling within subsection (1A) above, and

(e) the sample is taken before the end of the period of 24 hours starting with the time when his detention by virtue of this arrest for the first offence began.

(5D) A sample must not be taken from a person under this section if he is detained in a police station unless he has been brought before the custody office.][10]

[(6A) *The Secretary of State may by order made by statutory instrument amend subsection (3) above by substituting for the age for the time being specified a different age specified in the order.*

[(6A) The Secretary of State may by order made by statutory instrument amend—

(a) paragraph (a) of subsection (3) above, by substituting for the age for the time being specified a different age specified in the order, or different ages so specified for different police areas so specified;

(b) paragraph (b) of that subsection, by substituting for the age for the time being specified a different age specified in the order.][11]

(6B) A statutory instrument containing an order under subsection (6A) above shall not be made unless a draft of the instrument has been laid before, and approved by a resolution of, each House of Parliament.][12]

150

(7)   Information obtained form a sample taken under this section may be disclosed—

(a)   for the purposes of informing any decision about granting bail in criminal proceedings (within the meaning of the Bail Act 1976) to the person concerned;

[(aa) for the purpose of informing any decision about the giving of a conditional caution under Part 3 of the Criminal Justice Act 2003 to the person concerned;][13]

(b)   where the person concerned is in police detention or is remanded in or committed to custody by an order of a court or has been granted such bail, for the purpose of informing any decision about his supervision;

(c)   where the person concerned is convicted of an offence, for the purpose of informing any decision about the appropriate sentence to be passed by a court and any decision about his supervision or release;

[(ca) for the purpose of an assessment which the person concerned is required to attend by virtue of section 9(2) or 10(2) of the Drugs Act 2005;\

(cb)   for the purpose of proceedings against the person concerned for an offence under section 12(3) or 14(3) of that Act;][14]

(d)   for the purpose of ensuing that appropriate advice and treatment is made available to the person concerned.

[(9)   *In relation to a person who has not attained the age of 18, this section applies only where—*

(a)   *the relevant chief officer has been notified by the Secretary of State that arrangements for the taking of samples under this section from persons who have not attained the age of 18 have been made for the police area as a whole, or for the particular police station, in which the person is in police detention; and*

(b)   *the notice has not been withdrawn.*[15]

(10)   In this section—

"appropriate adult", in relation to a person who has not attained the age of 17, means—

(a)   his parent or guardian or, if he is in the care of a local authority or voluntary organisation, a person representing that authority or organisation; or

(b)   a social worker of a local authority [. . .][16]; or

(c)   if no person falling within paragraph (a) or (b) is available, any responsible person aged 18 or over who is not a police officer or a person employed by the police;

"relevant chief officer" means—

(a)   in relation to a police area, the chief officer of police of the police force for that police area; or

(b)   in relation to a police station, the chief officer of police of the police force for the police area in which the police station is situated.][17]]

NOTES

[1] Words substituted by Drugs Act 2005 (c.17), s.7(1), (2), (13), (14); amendment in force on a date to be appointed.

[2] Subsection inserted by Drugs Act 2005 (c.17), s.7(1), (3), (13), (14); amendment in force on a date to be appointed.

[3] Words substituted by Drugs Act 2005 (c.17), s.7(1), (4), (13), (14); amendment in force on a date to be appointed.

[4] Words substituted by Criminal Justice Act 2003 (c.44) s.5(1), (3)(a); amendment in force August 1, 2004 (in relation to Cleveland, Greater Manchester, Humberside, Merseyside, metropolitan police district, Nottinghamshire and West Yorkshire police areas), and on a date to be appointed for other purposes.

[5] Subsection substituted by Drugs Act 2005 (c.17), s.7(1), (5), (13), (14); amendment in force on a date to be appointed.

[6] Word substituted by Drugs Act 2005 (c.17), s.7(1), (6), (13), (14); amendment in force on a date to be appointed.

[7] Subsections inserted by Drugs Act 2005 (c.17), s.7(1), (7), (13), (14); amendments in force on a date to be appointed.

[8] Words inserted by Drugs Act 2005 (c.17), s.7(1), (8), (13), (14); amendment in force on a date to be appointed.

[9] Subsection inserted by Criminal Justice Act 2003 (c.44) s.5(1) (3)(b); amendment in force August 1, 2004 (in relation to Cleveland, Greater Manchester, Humberside, Merseyside, metropolitan police district, Nottinghamshire and West Yorkshire police areas), and on a date to be appointed for other purposes.

[10] Subsections inserted by Drugs Act 2005 (c.17), s.7(1), (9), (13), (14); amendments in force on a date to be appointed.

[11] Subsection substituted (new 6A) by Drugs Act 2005 (c.17), s.7(1), (10), (13), (14); amendments in force on a date to be appointed.

[12] Subsections inserted (old 6A, 6B) by Criminal Justice Act 2003 (c.44) s.5 (1), (3)(c); amendment in force August 1, 2004 (in relation to Cleveland, Greater Manchester, Humberside, Merseyside, metropolitan police district, Nottinghamshire and West Yorkshire police areas), and on a date to be appointed for other purposes.

[13] Subsection inserted by Drugs Act 2005 (c.17), s.7(1), (11), (13), (14); amendment in force on a date to be appointed.

[14] Subsections inserted by Drugs Act 2005 (c.17), s.23(1), Sch.1, paras 1, 4; amendments in force on a date to be appointed.

[15] Subsection repealed by Drugs Act 2005 (c.17), s.7(1), (12) to (14), 23(2), Sch.2; amendment in force on a date to be appointed.

[16] Words repealed by Children Act 2004 (c.31), s.64, Sch.5, Pt 4; amendment in force April 1, 2005.

[17] Subsections inserted by Criminal Justice Act 2003 (c.44) s.5(1), (3)(d); amendment in force August 1, 2004 (in relation to Cleveland, Greater Manchester, Humberside, Merseyside, metropolitan police district, Nottinghamshire and West Yorkshire police areas), and on a date to be appointed for other purposes.

[s 63C Testing for presence of Class A drugs—supplementary]

App–070

(1) A person guilty of an offence under section 63B above shall be liable on summary conviction to imprisonment for a term not exceeding [51 weeks][1], or to a fine not exceeding level 4 on the standard scale, or to both.

NOTE

[1] Words substituted by Criminal Justice Act 2003 (c.44), s.280(2), (3), Sch.26, para.35; amendment in force on a date to be appointed.

s 64 Destruction of fingerprints and samples

[(1A) Where—

  (a) fingerprints[, impressions of footwear][1] or samples are taken from a person in connection with the investigation of an offence, and

  (b) subsection (3) below does not require them to be destroyed,

the fingerprints[, impressions of footwear][2] or samples may be retained after they have fulfilled the purposes for which they were taken but shall not be used by any person except for purposes related to the prevention or detection of crime, the investigation of an offence[, the conduct of a prosecution or the identification of a deceased person or of the person from whom a body part came][3]

(1B) In subsection (1A) above—

  (a) the reference to using a fingerprint [or an impression of footwear][4] includes a reference to allowing any check to be made against it under section 63A(1) or (1C) above and to disclosing it to any person;

  (b) the reference to using a sample includes a reference to allowing any check to be made under section 63A(1) or (1C) above against it or against information derived from it and to disclosing it or any such information to any person;

  (c) the reference to crime includes a reference to any conduct which—

     (i) constitutes one or more criminal offences (whether under the law of a part of the United Kingdom or of a country or territory outside the United Kingdom); or

    (ii) is, or corresponds to, any conduct which, if it all took place in any one part of the United Kingdom, would constitute one or more criminal offences;

and

  (d) the references to an investigation and to a prosecution include references, respectively, to any investigation outside the United Kingdom of any crime or suspected crime and to a prosecution brought in respect of any crime in a country or territory outside the United Kingdom.]

[(1BA) Fingerprints taken from a person by virtue of section 61(6A) above must be destroyed as soon as they have fulfilled the purpose for which they are taken.][5]

(3) If—

  (a) fingerprints[, impressions of footwear][6] or samples are taken from a person in connection with the investigation of an offence; and

  (b) that person is not suspected of having committed the offence,

they must, [except as provided in [the following provisions of this section],] be destroyed as soon as they have fulfilled the purpose for which they were taken.

[(3AA) Samples [fingerprints and impressions of footwear][7] are not required to be destroyed under subsection (3) above if—

  (a) they were taken for the purposes of the investigation of an offence of which a person has been convicted; and

  (b) a sample[, fingerprint, (or as the case may be) an impression of footwear][8] was also taken from the convicted person for the purposes of that investigation.

(3AB) Subject to subsection (3AC) below, where a person is entitled under [subsection (1BA) or (3)][9] above to the destruction of any fingerprint[, impression of footwear][10] or sample taken from him (or would be but for subsection (3AA) above), neither the fingerprint[, nor the impression of footwear,][11] nor the sample, nor any information derived from the sample, shall be used—

(a)   in evidence against the person who is or would be entitled to the destruction of that fingerprint[, impression of footwear][12] or sample; or

(b)   for the purposes of the investigation of any offence;

and subsection (1B) above applies for the purposes of this subsection as it applies for the purposes of subsection (1A) above.

(3AC) Where a person from whom a fingerprint[, impression of footwear][13] or sample has been taken consents in writing to its retention—

(a)   that [fingerprint[, impression of footwear][14] or][15] sample need not be destroyed under subsection (3) above;

(b)   subsection (3AB) above shall not restrict the use that may be made of the fingerprint[, impression of footwear][16] or sample or, in the case of a sample, of any information derived from it; and

(c)   that consent shall be treated as comprising a consent for the purposes of section 63A(1C) above;

and a consent given for the purpose of this subsection shall not be capable of being withdrawn.

[This subsection does not apply to fingerprints taken from a person by virtue of section 61(6A) above.][17]

(3AD) For the purposes of subsection (3AC) above it shall be immaterial whether the consent is given at, before or after the time when the entitlement to the destruction of the fingerprint[, impression of footwear,][18] or sample arises.]

[(5)   If fingerprints [or impressions of footwear][19] are destroyed—

(a)   any copies of the fingerprints [or impressions of footwear][20] shall also be destroyed; and

(b)   any chief officer of police controlling access to computer data relating to the fingerprints [or impressions of footwear][21] shall make access to the data impossible, as soon as it is practicable to do so.]

(6)   A person who asks to be allowed to witness the destruction of his fingerprints [or impressions of footwear][22] or copies of them shall have a right to witness it.

[(6A) If—

(a)   subsection (5)(b) above falls to be complied with; and

(b)   the person to whose fingerprints [or impressions of footwear][23] the data relate asks for a certificate that it has been complied with,

such a certificate shall be issued to him, not later than the end of the period of three months beginning with the day on which he asks for it, by the responsible chief officer of police or a person authorised by him or on his behalf for the purposes of this section.

NOTES

1 and 2   Words inserted by Serious Organised Crime and Police Act 2005 (c.15), s.118(1), (4)(a); amendment in force on a date to be appointed.

3   Words substituted by Serious Organised Crime and Police Act 2005 (c.15), s.117(6), (7); amendment in force April 7, 2005.

⁴ Words inserted by Serious Organised Crime and Police Act 2005 (c.15), s.118(1), (4)(b); amendment in force on a date to be appointed.

⁵ Subsection inserted by Serious Organised Crime and Police Act 2005 (c.15), s.117(6), (8); amendment in force on a date to be appointed.

⁶ Words inserted by Serious Organised Crime and Police Act 2005 (c.15), s.118(1), (4)(c); amendment in force on a date to be appointed.

⁷ Words substituted by Serious Organised Crime and Police Act 2005 (c.15), s.118(1), (4)(d)(i); amendment in force on a date to be appointed.

⁸ Words substituted by Serious Organised Crime and Police Act 2005 (c.15), s.118(1), (4)(d)(ii); amendment in force on a date to be appointed.

⁹ Words substituted by Serious Organised Crime and Police Act 2005 (c.15), s.117(1), (9); amendment in force on a date to be appointed.

^{10 and 12} Words inserted by Serious Organised Crime and Police Act 2005 (c.15), s.118(1), (4)(e)(i); amendment in force on a date to be appointed.

¹¹ Words inserted by Serious Organised Crime and Police Act 2005 (c.15), s.118(1), (4)(e)(ii); amendment in force on a date to be appointed.

^{13, 14 and 16} Words inserted by Serious Organised Crime and Police Act 2005 (c.15), s.118(1), (4)(f); amendment in force on a date to be appointed.

¹⁵ Words inserted by Serious Organised Crime and Police Act 2005 (c.15), s.117(6), (10)(a); amendment in force on a date to be appointed.

¹⁷ Words inserted by Serious Organised Crime and Police Act 2005 (c.15), s.117(1), (10)(b); amendment in force on a date to be appointed.

¹⁸ Words inserted by Serious Organised Crime and Police Act 2005 (c.15), s.118(1), (4)(g); amendment in force on a date to be appointed.

^{19 to 21} Words inserted by Serious Organised Crime and Police Act 2005 (c.15), s.118(1), (4)(h); amendment in force on a date to be appointed.

²² Words inserted by Serious Organised Crime and Police Act 2005 (c.15), s.118(1), (4)(i); amendment in force on a date to be appointed.

²³ Words inserted by Serious Organised Crime and Police Act 2005 (c.15), s.118(1), (4)(j); amendment in force on a date to be appointed.

[s 64A Photographing of suspects etc

[(1A) A person falling with subsection (1B) below may, on the occasion of the relevant event referred to in subsection (1B), be photographed elsewhere than at a police station—   **App–072**

(a) with the appropriate consent; or

(b) if the appropriate consent is withheld or it is not practicable to obtain it, without it.

(1B) A person falls within this subsection if he has been—

(a) arrested by a constable for an offence;

(b) taken into custody by a constable after being arrested for an offence by a person other than a constable;

(c) made subject to a requirement to wait with a community support officer under paragraph 2(3) or (3B) of Schedule 4 to the Police Reform Act 2002 ("the 2002 Act");

(d) given a penalty notice by a constable in uniform under Chapter 1 of Part 1 of the Criminal Justice and Police Act 2001, a penalty notice by a constable under section 444A of the Education Act 1996, or a fixed penalty notice by a constable in uniform under section 54 of the Road Traffic Offenders Act 1988;

(e) given a notice in relation to a relevant fixed penalty offence (within the meaning of paragraph 1 of Schedule 4 to the 2002 Act) by a community support officer by virtue of a designation applying that paragraph to him; or

(f)   given a notice in relation to a relevant fixed penalty offence (within the meaning of paragraph 1 of Schedule 5 to the 2002 Act) by an accredited person by virtue of accreditation specifying that that paragraph applies to him.][1]

(4)   A photograph taken under this section—

(a)   may be used by, or disclosed to, any person for any purpose related to the prevention or detection of crime, the investigation of an offence or the conduct of a prosecution [or to the enforcement of a sentence][2]; and

(b)   after being so used or disclosed, may be retained but may not be used or disclosed except for a purpose so related.

(5)   In subsection (4)—

(a)   the reference to crime includes a reference to any conduct which—

(i)   constitutes one or more criminal offences (whether under the law of a part of the United Kingdom or of a country or territory outside the United Kingdom); or

(ii)   is, or corresponds to, any conduct which, if it all took place in any one part of the United Kingdom, would constitute one or more criminal offences;

and

(b)   the references to an investigation and to a prosecution include references, respectively, to any investigation outside the United Kingdom of any crime or suspected crime and to a prosecution brought in respect of any crime in a country or territory outside the United Kingdom; [and

(c)   "sentence" includes any order made by a court in England and Wales when dealing with an offender in respect of his offence.][3]

[(6A)   In this section, a "photograph" includes a moving image, and corresponding expressions shall be construed accordingly.][4]

[(7)   Nothing in this section applies to a person arrested under an extradition arrest power.][5]]

NOTES

[1] Subsections inserted by Serious Organised Crime and Police Act 2005 (c.15), s.116(1), (2); amendment in force on a date to be appointed.
[2] Words inserted by Serious Organised Crime and Police Act 2005 (c.15), s.116(1), (3); amendment in force on a date to be appointed.
[3] Paragraph inserted by Serious Organised Crime and Police Act 2005 (c.15), s.116(1), (4); amendment in force on a date to be appointed.
[4] Subsection inserted by Serious Organised Crime and Police Act 2005 (c.15), s.116(1), (5); amendment in force on a date to be appointed.
[5] Subsection inserted by Extradition Act 2003 (c.41), s.169(1), (5); amendment in force January 1, 2004.

s 65 Fingerprints and samples—supplementary

App–073   (1)   In this Part of this Act—

. . .

["extradition arrest power" means any of the following—

(a)   a Part 1 warrant (within the meaning given by the Extradition Act 2003) in respect of which a certificate under section 2 of that Act has been issued;

(b)   section 5 of that Act;

(c)   a warrant issued under section 71 of that Act;

[. . .]

(d)   a provisional warrant (within the meaning given by that Act)]¹;

. . .

["intimate sample" means—

(a)   a sample of blood, semen or any other tissue fluid, urine or pubic hair;

(b)   a dental impression;

[(c)   a swab taken from any part of a person's genitals (including pubic hair) or from a person's body orifice other than the mouth;]²

(d)   a swab taken from a person's body orifice other than the mouth];

. . .

["non-intimate sample" means—

(a)   a sample of hair other than pubic hair;

(b)   a sample taken from a nail on from under a nail;

[(c)   a swab taken from any part of a person's body other than a part from which a swab taken would be an intimate sample;]³

(d)   saliva;

(e)   a skin impression];

NOTES

¹ Definition inserted by Extradition Act 2003 (c.41), s.169(1), (6); amendment in force January 1, 2004.

² Words substituted by Serious Organised Crime and Police Act 2005 (c.15), s.119(1), (2); amendment in force July 1, 2005.

³ Words substituted by Serious Organised Crime and Police Act 2005 (c.15), s.119(1), (3); amendment in force July 1, 2005.

SCHEDULE 1

SPECIAL PROCEDURE

Making of orders by circuit [judge]

1. If on an application made by a constable a [judge]¹ is satisfied that one or other of the sets of access conditions is fulfilled, he may make an order under paragraph 4 below.   **App–074**

2. The first set of access conditions is fulfilled if—

(a)   there are reasonable grounds for believing—

(i)   that [an indictable offence][2] has been committed;

(ii)   that there is material which consists of special procedure material or includes special procedure material and does not also include excluded material on premises specified in the application[, or on premises occupied or controlled by a person specified in the application (including all such premises on which there are reasonable grounds for believing that there is such material as it is reasonably practicable so to specify)]][3];

(iii) that the material is likely to be of substantial value (whether by itself or together with other material) to the investigation in connection with which the application is made; and

(iv) that the material is likely to be relevant evidence;

(b)   other methods of obtaining the material—

(i)   have been tried without success; or

(ii)   have not been tried because it appeared that they

were bound to fail; and

(c)   it is in the public interest, having regard—

(i)   to the benefit likely to accrue to the investigation if the material is obtained; and

(ii)   to the circumstances under which the person in possession of the material holds it, that the material should be produced or that access to it should be given.

3. The second set of access conditions is fulfilled if—

(a)   there are reasonable grounds for believing that there is material which consists of or includes excluded material or special procedure material on premises specified in the application[, or on premises occupied or controlled by a person specified in the application (including all such premises on which there are reasonable grounds for believing that there is such material as it is reasonably practicable so to specify)][4];

(b)   but for section 9(2) above a search of [such premises][5] for that material could have been authorised by the issue of a warrant to a constable under an enactment other than this Schedule; and

(c)   the issue of such a warrant would have been appropriate.

4. An order under this paragraph is an order that the person who appears to the [judge][6] to be in possession of the material to which the application relates shall—

(a)   produce it to a constable for him to take away; or

(b)   give a constable access to it,

not later than the end of the period of seven date from the date of the order or the end of such longer period as the order may specify.

12. If on an application made by a constable a [judge][7]—

(a)   is satisfied—

(i)   that either set of access conditions is fulfilled [in relation to each set of premises specified in the application];[8] and

(ii)   that any of the further conditions set out in paragraph 14 below is also fulfilled; or

(b)   is satisfied—

(i)   that the second set of access conditions is fulfilled; and

    (ii)   that an order under paragraph 4 above relating to the material has not been complied with,

he may issue a warrant authorising a constable to enter and search the premises, [or (as the case may be) all premises occupied or controlled by the person referred to in paragraph 2(1)(ii) or 3(a) including such sets of premises as are specified in the application (an "all premises warrant")].[9]

[12A. The judge may not issue an all premises warrant unless he is satisfied—

    (a)   that there are reasonable grounds for believing that it is necessary to search premises occupied or controlled by the person in question which are not specified in the application, as well as those which are, in order to find the material in questions; and

    (b)   that it is not reasonably practicable to specify all the premises which he occupies or controls which might need to be searched.][10]

14. The further conditions mentioned in paragraph 12(a)(ii) above are—

    (a)   that it is not practicable to communicate with any person entitled to grant entry to the premises [. . .];[11]

    (b)   that it is practicable to communicate with a person entitled to grant entry to the premises but it is not practicable to communicate with any person entitled to grant access to the material;

    (c)   that the material contains information which—

        (i)   is subject to a restriction or obligation such as is mentioned in section 11(2)(b) above; and

        (ii)   is likely to be disclosed in breach of it if a warrant is not issued;

    (d)   that service of notice of an application for an order under paragraph 4 above may seriously prejudice the investigation.

15. (1)   If a person fails to comply with an order under paragraph 4 above, a [judge][12] may deal with him as if he had committed a contempt of the Crown Court.

    (2)   Any enactment relating to contempt of the Crown Court shall have effect in relation to such a failure as if it were such a contempt.

[17. [In this schedule "judge" means [a judge of the High Court, a Circuit judge, a Recorder][13] or a District Judge (Magistrates' Courts).][14]

NOTES

[1] Words substituted by Courts Act 2003 (c.39), s.65, Sch.4, para.6(1); amendment in force on a date to be appointed.

[2] Words substituted by Serious Organised Crime and Police Act 2005 (c.15), s.111, Sch.7, Pt 3, para.43(1), (13); amendment in force on a date to be appointed.

[3] Words inserted by Serious Organised Crime and Police Act 2005 (c.15), s.113(1), (10), (11); amendment in force on a date to be appointed.

[4] Words inserted by Serious Organised Crime and Police Act 2005 (c.15), s.113(1), (10), (11); amendment in force on a date to be appointed.

[5] Words inserted by Serious Organised Crime and Police Act 2005 (c.15), s.113(1), (10), (12); amendment in force on a date to be appointed.

[6] Words substituted by Courts Act 2003 (c.39), s.65, Sch.4, para.6(1); amendment in force on a date to be appointed.

[7] Words substituted by Courts Act 2003 (c.39), s.65, Sch.4, para.6(1); amendment in force on a date to be appointed.

[8] Words inserted by Serious Organised Crime and Police Act 2005 (c.15), s.113(1), (10), (13)(a); amendment in force on a date to be appointed.

[9] Words inserted by Serious Organised Crime and Police Act 2005 (c.15), s.113(1), (10), (13)(b); amendment in force on a date to be appointed.

[10] Paragraph inserted by Serious Organised Crime and Police Act 2005 (c.15), s.113(1), (10), (14); amendment in force on a date to be appointed.

[11] Words repealed by Serious Organised Crime and Police Act 2005 (c.15), ss.113(1), (10), (15), 174(2), Sch.17, Pt 2; amendment in force on a date to be appointed.

[12] Words substituted by Courts Act 2003 (c.39), s.65, Sch.4, para.6(1); amendment in force on a date to be appointed.

[13] Words substituted by Serious Organised Crime and Police Act 2005 (c.15), s.114(1), (9); amendment in force on a date to be appointed.

[14] Paragraph inserted by Courts Act 2003 (c.39), Sch.4 para.6(2); amendment in force on a date to be appointed.

Index